Beyond the
Breakwater

Beyond the Breakwater

Memories of Home

CATHERINE FOLEY

MERCIER PRESS

IRISH PUBLISHER – IRISH STORY

MERCIER PRESS
Cork
www.mercierpress.ie

© Catherine Foley, 2018

ISBN: 978 1 78117 546 0

10 9 8 7 6 5 4 3 2 1

A CIP record for this title is available from the British Library

Printed and bound in the EU.

Contents

Preface   9

WATERFORD CITY & PASSAGE EAST

1	Games We Used To Play	16
2	At Play	20
3	My Mother's Mandolin	24
4	My Grandmother, the Tailoress	27
5	Daddy Walsh	30
6	Passage	34
7	Listening to the Hoover	37
8	Saying Goodnight to Our Lady	40
9	Doing Alphonsus Road	43
10	Annie Brophy	46
11	Tall as a Mountain was He	51
12	Nuns	54
13	Jackie Kennedy in Woodstown	57
14	The River Suir Runs Through It	60
15	Geneva Barracks	64
16	Feeding the Birds	67
17	Newfoundland	70

RING

18	Moving	76
19	Mouse	83
20	A Dog Named Jingle	86
21	Joe	89
22	Sheila	93
23	Harold	96

24   Boarding School   99

25   Boys   102

26   Summer Songs   105

27   Swan Song   108

28   My Aunts   111

29   The Boys from Bagenalstown   114

30   Sisters   119

31   The Pope's Visit   120

32   Nana Mouskouri   123

33   Mario Lanzo   126

34   A Gentleman Caller   129

35   The Helvick Summer   133

36   Tribal Dance   139

37   Finals   143

THE GREAT WIDE WORLD

38   My First Interview   148

39   The Boys of 2F   152

40   Secrets of a Lost Diary   155

41   Praying in Prague   158

42   The Green Ray   161

43   In a Train   164

44   The Two Germans   166

45   Angela   170

46   Gypsy King   174

47   My Street   179

48   In Mick O'Dea's Studio   184

49   Frawley's   188

50   Crogal   192

51   Dusty Books   195

52   Guatemala   199

53   The Berber Women   203

54	Haworth	208
55	The Basin Street Visitor	212
56	Joe Martell	215
57	Rome	220
58	The Diary of a Social Columnist	224

RETURN

59	The Missing Painting	230
60	Theatre Royal	233
61	The Premiere	237
62	Ardkeen Visit	240
63	Ballast	248
64	Christmas by the Graves	249
65	Respite	252
66	Dan, the Man	255
67	Nudes	258
68	The SS *Kincora*	261
69	Romance in the Air	264
70	Following the Wren	268
71	Fairies on Woodstown Strand	270
72	Graveyard	271
73	A Kaleidoscope of Days	274
74	When Walls Grow Cold	276
75	Midnight Mass	279

| Acknowledgements | 284 |

In memory of my parents
Ena and Joe Foley,
and with gratitude to my sisters
RoseAnn and Miriam.

Preface

When we lived in Waterford city I was a quiet little girl who wore frocks, sandals and white socks. My fringe fell like a curtain over my forehead. I stood quietly to listen when spoken to. I kept my feet together and, if we had visitors, I sat with my hands together in my lap. I remember playing with my dolls behind my mother's chair in the kitchen, or having fun in the garden with my two young sisters, until I got a bit older and I was tempted out by the neighbouring children who skipped and hopscotched on our street's large slate footpaths.

We lived on an elegant street known as Lower Newtown, in one of its terraced three-storey Edwardian houses. These were tall and dour, peering over lower houses across the street. The People's Park was out of sight but it wasn't far away. From the attic in our house we could see slated roofs, terracotta chimney pots, church spires and turreted towers. In the back garden we were pencilled in by laurel hedges and tiled passageways, stone steps and wrought-iron railings.

On the street, chalk was used to mark out boxes on the footpath: we'd hop away all morning, going from box number one to three to five to nine, then turning to go again. If it rained, the boxes washed away and we were called in. The grey sky would turn to navy and the drops would pour steadily onto the city. After the rain, boys and girls ran out and once again chased each other from gateway to gateway, step to step, corner to corner.

On sunny days, we had tea-sets to play with in the garden and we chatted through a hole in the hedge with the neighbours.

We poured imaginary tea for each other, passing little blue cups and make-believe sandwiches back and forth.

'Oh, do have another one.'

'Oh, I couldn't possibly.'

Where did those mimicking voices of urbanity and civility come from? Like others living near us, we had private piano and elocution lessons.

My mother and father went out each Saturday night to meet friends, dressing up and standing at the hall door to say good-night to us. Often in the care of our grandfather, we watched them from the landing, starry-eyed with love and longing to be taken along.

When we still lived in the city we got a black-and-white television. It banished the sounds of the wind that I used to hear whistling and shrieking through the hallway just outside the dining room. The television inured us to the cold. It drew us in, distracting us from the starry sky outside that arched over the long, narrow gardens in parallel rows at the back of our houses. Once the television was turned on, our eyes grew round, our breathing stilled and we became quieter. We no longer looked outside at the darkening evening. We settled into chairs and watched silently as the cleverness and magic of it unfolded. We started to tune in to its messages of movement and speech, attracted by the flickering screen where characters such as a cartoon duck called Daithí Lacha held us in thrall; where an animated pair from Poland named Lolek and Bolek popped and paraded like match-sticks in front of our mesmerised eyes; and where Daniel Boone, the American frontiersman of the eponymous action adventure series, kept us tense and separate from everything around us.

At weekends, we'd leave the city behind us and drive south

along the river to my mother's home place some eight miles away. Passage East, on the banks of the Suir, was where my grandparents lived and to us it seemed as if it was always filled with sunshine, fuelled by freedom and peopled by giants. While we were there we became part of the village's tightly knit fishing community. We knew every laneway and square. We'd be taken down to the strand to play and on our way we'd run along the cockle walk and out along the breakwater to look at the boats going out to sea, or coming home with their catch at the end of the day. Families depended on those catches and I still remember the constant questions that returning fishermen were asked: did ye catch any salmon today, what time is high tide, or are ye going out again today? Those days in Passage East helped shape my understanding of what it meant to live by the sea. At the end of our visit, we'd say our goodbyes and pile into our Mini and my mother, who learned to drive before my father, would drive us back to the city.

Then, one day, my two aunts arrived with an idea for my parents, one that would change my family's life forever. Their car pulled up outside our house in Lower Newtown, where we were playing outside, acting like raggedy urchins. We all stopped to stare at the posh car as the two women we hardly knew went through our gate to knock at our door. Once inside and settled, they suggested to my father that he should consider moving the family to the Ring Peninsula – or its Irish translation, An Rinn – a place that he and his siblings loved as they'd spent all their summer holidays there as children because it had been their father's wish that they learn Irish. So each year they rented a cottage, settled in and immersed themselves in the life of the Gaeltacht community. As well as learning to speak Irish like the local people, they also formed lifelong bonds with many of them, and they fell in love with the music, the traditions and the freedom they had. To them Ring was Shangri-La, Tír na nÓg and Paradise all rolled into one.

My aunts knew that my father had almost had a stroke and that he'd been given a warning by his doctor to change his high-pressure job as a manager in Stanley's Waterford Iron Foundry, the doctor arguing that he needed something less stressful. So, after much discussion, my parents agreed to sell our house in Waterford and move to this Irish-speaking area in the furthest corner of the county, a lush promontory of land that juts out into the sea. We all looked on this move as a great new adventure. By this time my grandparents in Passage East had passed away, so we didn't feel like we were leaving anyone behind. Us children had no sense of fear or trepidation and my mother was happy once she was with my father and we were all together as a family.

Overnight, we went from a city to a rural environment, from gazing hungrily at the television to a place where everyone's house was imbued with the shadows and smells of long ago. We left our urban, convent-educated, nine-to-five sensibility – a routine where Dada came home to his dinner each day from the foundry – to, instead, living a life of earthy complexity, one where we embraced an archaic and anarchic lifestyle.

In Ring I felt the ground shift underneath me. After the prism of our black-and-white television, everything was suddenly in glorious technicolour. As we settled in the village of Baile na nGall, I saw a neighbour running awkwardly through a field of cow-dung after his cows; I saw wild boys jumping off the pier into the sea in an explosion of exuberance and devilment; and I heard Irish words and phrases that plucked on heart strings I never knew existed. I felt myself slip towards wildness, towards strangeness and volatility.

Ever since, I've been trying to reconcile the two worlds of my youth: the powerful pull of my early childhood years in the city, and my teenage years in a different, more starkly beautiful landscape with a different culture and a different language, where life is deeply felt and steeped in the poetry of the past.

Life in Ring undoubtedly captured me whole. Every summer, there was beauty in every direction – white daisies speckled the fields, blue sky and sea stretched like music off into limitless air and boats moved over the sea, fluttering into and out of our range like butterflies. Black bobbing heads in the waves were seals coming up to say hello. Green ferns waved on hillsides; furze glinted in sunlight. The roads that wound upwards from our house, winding around bends and corners, spellbound us into a trance-like silence.

When autumn came in An Rinn we became watchful of time, of leaves falling, night coming, bells ringing, cows sloping, cars revving, feet shuffling, dogs barking and fires crackling. At Halloween we used to smear paint across our faces and dress up in old clothes to go walking along the boreens, knocking on doors in search of thrills and money. We were frightened out of our wits by the sounds and shadows we heard and saw along the way in the depths of those late October nights. We felt and sensed our way along the roads, going with our hearts in our mouths, tripping over our grown-up overcoats and skirts, blinded by gold poster paints in our eyes and hysterical with fear of the unexpected. Those nights were full of screams and flight up to the point when we staggered home, still blind and feeling our way, trembling and exhilarated in turn by terror or delight.

Through all the seasons music wafted in from the sitting room to our kitchen when visiting friends, aunts or uncles and sometimes our father sang verses or snippets of Irish songs, old notes that echoed down the centuries.

For me, the pull of the city, combined with my mother's place of Passage East, has always tugged away with and against the powerful draw of An Rinn and the ancient world that the Irish language represents. Even after my travels as an adult and my time away, my mind still returns to the same questions – am I part of an ongoing tradition, or was I a blank slate ready to be written on like the slates of my street in Waterford? Am I a mariner? A fisherwoman? A Gaeilgeoir? Am I a traditionalist who is earth-rooted and bound to an ancient, dying language, or am I civilised and sanitised by modernity and the progress of time? Am I here or am I there? Which side of the divide do I cross to? Or am I perhaps a bridge between the two?

An airy day often gets me thinking about the passing of time and those who have passed away. After the death of my parents, the gnawing loss and loneliness often leaves me with a sense of something missing. But when I sit on a wall in the evening light if I'm out for a walk, I sometimes think back and I feel closer to them. I hope the stories contained in this book, which track the arc of my life through the prism of my memories – first as a child, then as a teenager and finally as an adult – will make you smile, and possibly rekindle some memories of your own from an earlier time.

Waterford City
&
Passage East

I

Games We Used To Play

To get to our street of Lower Newtown from the city centre you had to pass over the Pill, a small tributary of the River Suir. You'd go up towards the old infirmary and on to the top of John's Hill. Then you'd turn left onto Percy Terrace and down you came to Lower Newtown. We lived across from Christ Church National School, which we all referred to merely as the 'Protestant school'.

Our street was made up of young families mixed in with some elderly neighbours. We played with all the neighbouring children, but especially the Chesters and the Keanes. Games always started out in a nice, civilised fashion. If someone had a bit of chalk and a couple of stones we'd play hopscotch along the footpath, or if we had two small bouncy balls, we'd play a game up against a wall, each of us taking turns to throw the balls against the wall, all the time singing out our verses as quickly as we could in time to the smack of the ball:

Dash it, Mrs Brown, Dash it Mrs Brown,
Dashey, dashey, dashey, dashey,
Dashey, Mrs Brown.
Over, Mrs Brown, Over Mrs Brown,
Over, over, over, over,
Over, Mrs Brown.
Under, Mrs Brown, Under Mrs Brown ...

Games We Used To Play

Whoever played had to maintain a certain rhythm and have good hand–eye co-ordination, moving deftly to catch one ball and throw the other until one of the balls dropped. The rest of us would wait, biding our time until an opening appeared. Then we'd step in quickly for a turn.

When it was my turn, I'd jump into the space and have a go. All eyes watched jealously, waiting to see when or how soon I'd drop the balls. When I did, the next girl was ready to push me out. 'I'm next,' she'd cry and elbow me away.

We had plenty of verses to accompany this game against the wall. Sometimes we'd all sing together like a Greek chorus gathered around the main player. Sometimes the ball juggler alone would recite the lines:

> *When I am dead*
> *And in my grave*
> *And all my bones are rotten,*
> *These two balls will tell you my age*
> *When I am quite forgotten.*
> *One, two, three, four, five, six, seven, eight,*
> *And now I'm on my second game.*

And that was how the day would tick by. There was always an audience when we played with a skipping rope. The group would stand in a tight circle and chant out the rhyme, sometimes clapping out the beat too in a taut countdown. Everyone counted the successful skips.

I look back on those days in Waterford through the zoetrope of time and I remember how we were, when all you longed to do was to jump into the middle and skip to the growing beat of the pack and the elegant belt of the rope.

Teddy Bear, Teddy Bear, tip the ground,
Teddy Bear, Teddy Bear, turn all around.
Teddy Bear, Teddy Bear, tie your shoe,
Teddy Bear, Teddy Bear, I love you.

Teddy Bear, Teddy Bear, pick up sticks,
Teddy Bear, Teddy Bear, switch off the lights.

The stakes were high, the rhyme ruled and you were sure to trip if you lost the pulse. Breathless, we'd jump with the arc of the rope swinging over us and with the space underneath our feet getting tighter. As the rope went faster, it slapped down like a metronome against the stones on the road.

The most difficult and best part was when a few of us skipped together as one, jumping over the rope and ducking our heads under, our bodies held in together, our feet pulled up as the rope swung over us. When as many of us as could fit – eight sometimes or even more – all jumped together under the one arc, singing the chant, breathless, the great slap of our feet together on the footpath and the jostling of elbows was magnificent.

In Waterford our streets rang with the drumbeat of half-truths, messages and hidden taboos. Our games were threaded with snippets of adult stories – something that was likely repeated throughout the country. Even the Clancy Brothers with Tommy Makem on an album they recorded in Carnegie Hall in 1963 sang about the chants they used to sing in Carrick-on-Suir as children:

Ahem, ahem, me mother's gone to church.
She told me not the play with you
Because you're in the dirt.

Games We Used To Play

It isn't because you're dirty,
It's not because you're clean,
It's because you have the whooping cough
And eat margarine.

Although only children, we in Lower Newtown were cruel sometimes, viscerally caught up in the pack dynamics of our street games. It was out and out war when enmity between one patch and another erupted. One night, after being assailed by a marauding horde from Alphonsus Road, we faced the group down in the laneway behind Percy Terrace, moving as one tribal and territorial unit towards them. Some of us threw stones to repel them. We were living viragoes, unafraid and shaking with excitement. It was the same principal as skipping; you couldn't miss the beat. You stepped up when your turn came.

My ankle was pumping blood when I got home that evening. When my mother opened the front door, I practically fainted into her arms with the excitement and the fright of our skirmish. I still bear the tiny scar from that stone on my ankle today and it reminds me of how I once was, territorial and driven by the beat of balls and feet and a skipping rope.

2

At Play

The scarlet quilt often slid off the brass bed and when it did it was like an invitation to play. We were mesmerised by that silky coverlet when it slithered off soundlessly and fell to the floor.

That quilt had all the grandeur and elegance of a ceremonial robe and when it was draped around our shoulders we could become anything. Pretending to say Mass was one of the games we played when we were small. We played it upstairs in the attic. No one heard our nonsense talk or our cries of pain when I pinched a leg or an arm, or was pinched myself.

Once draped in the quilt, the magic began in earnest. I, being the eldest – aged about seven at the time – generally took the lead, while my younger sisters, Miriam and RoseAnn, became my minions. 'Go down on your knees,' I'd instruct. 'In the name of the Father and the Son and the Holy Ghost,' I'd then intone, standing in front of my kneeling congregation. Generally, they kept their heads bowed and stayed silent like penitential sinners.

I'd hold aloft the silver cup my father had won some years before for rowing. The cup was a perfect stand-in for the chalice at Mass, heavily ornamented and engraved. Lowering it to the dressing table, I'd pass out imaginary Holy Communion wafers, moving gravely from one to the other. 'Body of Christ,' I'd say as I put my fingers on their protruding tongues. 'Amen,' Miriam would say before bowing her head and blessing herself in perfect imitation of all the parishioners we'd seen do it at Mass.

At Play

'Amen,' RoseAnn would repeat as she followed the synchronised movements. We'd stay up in the attic playing like that until our mother called us for our tea.

Sometimes Mama would get us ready early in the morning for a trip to her home place in Passage East. She'd bundle us into the car and off we'd set. We'd watch every twist and turn of the old road from the rear seat. We knew all the landmarks along the way. As we headed out the Dunmore road we'd notice the brass cock weathervane on an old steeple. Once on the Cheekpoint road, we'd wait to see the old bridge at Jack Meade's pub. When we saw the river, and the road began to hug the cliff in parts, twisting dramatically downhill towards the village at the mouth of the estuary, we'd try to keep our excitement in check until we saw Ballyhack across the river. We'd know then that we were drawing close. The sky overhead was always satin white and full of brightness, and we'd sit up eagerly in the car waiting to round the final bend in the road. 'I see Gran's house!' one of us would pipe up, pipping the other two to the post. Like kittens scratching and mewling, we'd push and elbow each other in the car, as much a way of communicating as it was a way to establish a hierarchy.

Gran kept empty cardboard boxes of Daz, Sweet Afton, salt, soap, old bottles of Jeyes Fluid and shoe polish for us and we'd play shop in her window, using matches for money. I, of course, was the shop owner. 'Yes, thank you, that's three pence, please. And here's your change. A hay-penny.'

'Thank you,' Miriam would say.

Then I'd call RoseAnn up.

'Pretend you want to buy some rashers. Here's your money … Oh, hello, Mrs Connors.'

'Hello, Mrs Foley. Isn't it very cold? Have you got any rashers?'

'I have. That's two shillings, please. Thank you.'

Back at home in Lower Newtown, we'd wrap our dog, Jingle, in a doll's blanket and put him in the pram as a substitute baby. He didn't like it because it was quite difficult for him to jump out of the old pram with its high-nelly-style wheels and its hood that came up like the back of an old-fashioned carriage, but we tended to ignore his looks of puzzlement and fright from under the blanket.

'Hello, Mrs Chester,' Miriam would say, pushing the pram down the garden path.

'Oh, isn't he a lovely baby?' I'd answer.

'Oh, Mrs Foley. You'll have to excuse me. I have to go and change his nappy,' she'd say.

'Oh, not at all, Mrs Chester. I understand. Is that what the smell is?'

We often played beside a little hole in the hedge and talked to the two Sherry children who lived next door, passing cutlery and plastic cups and saucers to each other, inviting each other to pretend tea parties. The hole was low down in the hedge and satisfyingly circular, like the porthole in a ship.

Mostly our play was make-believe but we did hairdressing for real. We all had long silky hair and we could plait it, clip it, part it and put rollers in it. Miriam in particular had lovely long, golden curls. We knew too that an appointment with the hairdresser was an event in our mother's life, especially if it was with Séamus, who had an upstairs salon on the quay. His name was whispered in reverential tones, especially if a particularly severe or risqué hairdo was causing compliments and comments. 'Who cut your hair? It's terrific.' He was a demigod in Waterford, deemed to be an artist with a pair of scissors, which he bore lightly and deftly. We all dreamed of being as skilled.

Was that why Miriam and I went behind the couch with the scissors one day? Perhaps we had an inkling it was dangerous, but we hunkered down, hidden, and I set about re-styling her hair. I modelled myself on Séamus, confident and quick, a snip here and a tug there until I cut off curls galore and one long, blond ringlet in particular that hung down over her back. It slipped down onto the floor between our knees.

Overcome with the startling consequence of these tiny snips, we stayed quiet until teatime. To make amends we set about polishing the edges of the floor around the room that were not covered by carpet. So industrious and thorough was I that I used the full tin of polish, much to my mother's frustration. But this infringement was nothing compared to her shock when she saw Miriam's shorn head of curls. They had to be trimmed severely back. Sadly, she never had long curls again – her hair has remained silky but straight to this day.

3

My Mother's Mandolin

Early nights in Waterford have merged into a general blur –
apart from the night we broke my mother's mandolin, an old
instrument with reddened wood and a resonance that she loved.
It remains clear in my mind still.

We were breathless and hot from reckless jumping from bed
to bed in our bedroom, flying across a great gap between the
beds, as well as flying across the slippery linoleum-covered floor.
The beds moved, shifting slightly each time as we landed. Earlier
we had played with my mother's mandolin but we'd discarded
it and it lay there that bedtime, hidden in the bedclothes at the
foot of one of the beds. Everything stopped, however, when
a foot landed awkwardly on the mandolin's neck and the old
instrument broke in two.

My mother used to pick out tunes on it. The rarity and
fragility of those tremolo pickings made that fateful twang of
the broken instrument all the more terrifying. The sound of the
wood breaking in two was like a stab wound.

We sat in our pyjamas, unsure what to do, until we heard
Mama's step on the stairs. Instinctively I ran to better hide
the broken thing. It was like a wounded animal, whimpering,
jangling and quivering still when I put it in the wardrobe and
ran back to the bed. We got in under the covers and waited for
Mama to come up and tuck us in.

'Are ye asleep yet?' she said as she came in.

My Mother's Mandolin

I felt seismic vibrations coming from the mandolin in the wardrobe – it was like a clanging bell demanding to be heard. She put the light out and came into the darkened room. If the light was left on, she would surely have seen the secret written plainly on my face. I felt myself blushing but I lay still in the semi-darkness when she came over to put the cold dab of holy water on each of our foreheads.

'Night,' she said.

'Night, Mama,' we sang like angels.

That night stays with me still. The guilt of my duplicity is etched on my heart. I remember how it preyed on me during the night, eating into my heart, while the mandolin lay broken and accusing in the wardrobe, crying out to be discovered.

I knew it would be like the whispered secret that surrounded the fabled King Labhraí Loingseach and his donkey's ears. I'd learned his story at school, how no one was ever allowed to speak of King Labhraí's donkey's ears on pain of death and how his secret remained unspoken until the barber who cut the king's hair – unable to keep the story to himself any longer – whispered the king's secret into a yew tree. Of course, when the tree was cut down and shaped into a harp for the king's bard, the music it played over and over again was a song about King Labhraí's donkey ears. As with that story, the truth of the broken mandolin would come out eventually.

Maybe our dread of the mandolin's discovery in the wardrobe was worse than the actual event itself. A couple of nights later, my mother opened the wardrobe suspiciously, watching our reaction.

'Have ye put something in here?' she asked.

Our faces had given the game away long before. She didn't punish us at all. She didn't even raise her voice.

'It's just one of those things,' she said, tucking us in and telling us to go to sleep. And isn't it strange that in all the years of adulthood and all the Christmases of plenty and generosity, I never thought to buy her a mandolin to replace the one we broke. And it's sad to think that she never owned another instrument ever again.

4

My Grandmother, the Tailoress

My maternal grandmother, Mary Ellen Walsh, was a tailoress who lived in Passage East all her life. She wore her grey hair tied back in a bun at the base of her head and had deep-set, dark-brown eyes – a link to her Corsican ancestors. She wore a navy wrap-around apron that had a pocket at the front in which she carried her beads, a few stray hairpins, sometimes the stub of a pencil or a spool of thread, and maybe a little ironed handkerchief.

Before I was born, Granny Walsh made beautiful taffeta dresses, camel-hair coats and tweed costumes for my mother. She did alterations and invisible mending, and she used patterns and photographs to make garments on request too.

When we were small she made all our clothes for us – little summer dresses of apple green or speckled orange with broderie anglaise bodices and white Peter Pan collars. Our dresses were always decorated with pockets and bows, and with buttons and fasteners. She'd also often insert pleats or attach a belt at the back, just to entertain us, her youngest patrons.

I remember how she started the Singer sewing machine by pressing down on the pedal underneath and then giving the wheel at her side a bit of a push. With nicely timed and precise movements, she'd crank up the machine and it would trundle into action, the needle ratcheting along. Then my grandmother's highly controlled and beautifully intense dance would begin in earnest – her upper body curving over the machine as she swayed back and forth in time with the motion of the wheel and the foot pedal underneath. She was perfectly aligned to the machine and always had it work with clockwork-like co-ordination.

The noise of the Singer had a rhythmic beat that carried a message of great conviction and certitude, both satisfying and mesmerising. It was like hearing an instrument of percussion or little hammer blows falling, cascading and tumbling down through the needle onto the fabric.

In the midst of this mechanical mayhem, she'd sometimes give the wheel at her side an extra little encouraging lash of her hand to speed up the sewing and that's when she'd travel into the stratosphere of sewing wizardry. And I'd sit spellbound in the room, caught up in the wonderful weave and weft of her world.

With her head bent low and her hands over the dress, she'd be flying along, concentrating fiercely, united as one with the powerful engine, her needle jabbing in and out of the material. At such moments, she was completely focused, having to keep the seam in its correct place, the pressure up and the momentum going, pacing it, weaving it, all the parts moving in one great headlong rush. She was the seamstresses' version of *Zen and the Art of Motorcycle Maintenance*: as that 1970s book also involved the propulsion of a machine and provided the reader with an opportunity to look at life and examine the fundamental questions of existence.

The Singer used to sound exhausted as it wound down, the frantic energy seeming to dissipate while my gran readjusted the fabric and fixed it under the needle. Then I'd see her thread the needle, holding her breath, her glasses halfway down her nose as she tried to hold the cotton between her thumb and forefinger and direct it through the eye. Then, it seemed as if she was doing battle with the eye of the needle and a dual of two wits ensued until she'd successfully threaded the needle and once again was able to bend the automaton to her will.

After this temporary stop was over, she'd give the wheel a little push, press down on the foot pedal and away she'd go, her feet going hell for leather, up and down, up and down, the action gloriously steady and definite. Sometimes I used to climb in under her legs and wait for a chance to sit on the pedal and get a ride on its sea-saw plate.

Now, when I cut through fabric or pull a piece of material flat on a table to consider its options, my deft hands flatten and fix, as if I already know what I'm going to do with the stuff. I realise then that I must be channelling my grandmother and her skill with a needle and thread.

5

Daddy Walsh

I remember my grandfather's hands, cupped one over the other and dry like rice-paper, and how he'd rub them together in anticipation of a visit to the pub with my father or a walk across the village for a chat with his friends, who paced slowly up and down the 'Men's Walk', that particular spot in the village which was their own place and where they could meet to discuss affairs of state and other manly topics.

My grandfather smoked Player's Navy Cut cigarettes. I still see him sitting at the kitchen table, picking stray strands of tobacco from the cigarette and tapping its top and tail against the packet, neatening it before his nicotine-stained fingers struck the match and a great flame burst forth.

He'd hold the flaming match and the cigarette up close between his hand and mouth, sheltering it while he drew in the fire. He'd keep going until he heard the tobacco crackle. Then with a great flourish, he'd quench the flame and inhale. For my entertainment he'd make rings with the smoke, creating *pock*, *pock* sounds with his mouth as he released the smoke, and we'd watch the circles wafting off into the air. He'd remain still then, perhaps looking out to sea, resting his right hand on his knee, the cigarette between two fingers, smoke curling up from it.

I was his first grandchild. When I was small, he'd take me in his arms and go to the high stone wall that bordered my grandparents' back garden to look in the ivy for a toffee lollipop, which he said the fairies had left for me. I called him 'Daddy Walsh', a name that became one of the familiar, comforting and musical sounds of home, the Walsh spoken as if it was spelt with an 'e' in the middle. *Welsh*.

Before he became a pilot on the River Suir, directing the boats up and down the estuary through the tricky currents and sand banks that lay between Dunmore East and the port of Waterford, he was a merchant seaman. He used to wear a black peaked cap, his matching black suit coat tight about his slight body, and so the uniformed sea captain on his packet of cigarettes always seemed so appropriate to my childish eyes. He wore the same cap and gold buttons; those sparkling blue eyes in the picture, with an old-fashioned sailing ship in the background, looked just like my Daddy Walsh.

He was a meticulously neat and methodical man, a dapper dresser who wore long black trousers with deep turn-ups and creases down the middle. They were always voluminously wide, like a mariner's trousers should be. The suits he wore were always black worn over a white shirt but I never saw him as a black-suited figure.

It was rare to see him standing with his braces hanging down or without a tie on or with his starched collar untied. As he grew frail towards the end, I remember him coming downstairs like this once, almost unmanned by the necessity of looking for help. I stood on the second step of the stairs in order to reach up and put the little stud in at the back of his shirt, thereby securing the old-fashioned detachable collar. It was a shock to me that he could no longer do it for himself.

I sometimes heard the scrape of the razor over his chin as he shaved. He wore black-laced shoes, which shone, buffed to a polished sheen. I remember his bushy eyebrows and how there was a sort of lop-sided tilt to his mouth when he smiled.

I think he had a sense of fun. I remember a twinkle in his eye, a skip in his step and a wide, big-lipped grin that was full of humour and charm. He loved to intrigue and mystify us with a riddle or a puzzling word conundrum. He loved a game of cards, too, and I recall him splicing and knotting ropes and sculpting small bits of wood.

He'd take me out to show me the village of Ballyhack across the river, Duncannon further down the coast and the Hook Head lighthouse off in the distance. Turning back, he'd show me Passage East itself, pointing out the Blind Quay, Canacanoe Hill, the remains of the fish factory and the cockle walk.

I remember the ceremony of each of my grandfather's acts, whether it was shaving, smoking or working with his ropes and wood. There was a delicate timing and deftness to each gesture; his movements were flowing and sure, like a dance. He didn't rush – whether he was drinking his tea, peeling a potato, or putting the brake on my pram, each act was carefully executed, just as he must have been on the river, guiding schooners and tankers, tug boats and container ships up and down the estuary channel.

This slowness was not to do with the stiff deliberate movements of his increasing age. It had to do with his being from another time, before phones, before television, before the dawn of modern technology. It was a time when semaphore – the art of signalling with flags – was still in use, when the chapel bell marking the time had a central place in daily lives. It was a time when Daddy Walsh, walking up the hill to the neighbouring townland of Crooke, was a traveller traversing his kingdom of Passage East, going from its heart to one of its outposts.

Daddy Walsh

Days were more sacred and slower. Time was apportioned each day and those portions were rarely altered. There was Mass time, dinner time, tea time, supper time. As the tidal river ebbed and flowed, there was full tide, high tide, low tide and 'it's gone out'. The year had its parts too, divided into segments such as winter time, summer time, Easter time, Lent. There was the salmon season and the herring season – the late evenings, the bright mornings, the cold nights, the dark nights.

When my grandfather left the house each day to stand in the shade of the Men's Walk, it was a different world, a more ordered world. It was a time when to be taken for a walk by my grandfather was an occasion, a ritual to be recorded for posterity.

6

Passage

Their words are in my head today,
they echo back and forth
lulling me into a half-remembered time,
when I was four and younger
in my pram
outside on the footpath
looking up at Canacanoe Hill.

The breakwater, the chapel, Woodstown, Ballyhack,
The Hooke, Crooke, Duncannon, Passage East.
I see Gran's house; I'm the first.

Passage waited for us,
The sky, streaked with lipstick,
turned satin in the evening light.
Moll Ruck, Mrs Bulger, Daddy Walsh, Maggie.
We grew up but their words are in my head today,

Gran, Ena, Uncle Joe,
do you see the lighthouse?
Mind the current,
the tide's coming in,
they're down on the breakwater.
Sugar spilled on the linoleum.
That was before when we lived up at the Gap.
Rogers' house, Rosie's house,
Patsy Barron over and back on the ferry

Passage

to Ballyhack where his amputated leg was buried
and the boats on their way up the Suir to Waterford
had to pass between his legs ever after.

The pump in front of Connors' house.
The shop, ice cream,
Did they get a salmon?
No, they're very scarce.
Crabs, gulls, stones, herrings.
The smoke house, shells, rain.
Get up to bed,
rosary beads behind the cushion on Gran's chair.
Mama sing-songing Gran's lines,
reminding us how she had frightened them as children
with her recitations in a ghostly voice:
'Sister Anne, Sister Anne, is there anyone comin'?
No-one comin' but the wind blowin', the grass growin'
An' two men on a horseback.'

Hurry up or we'll be late for Mass
Frocks-cardigans-sandals, ribbons-clips-lipstick-powder,
The Angelus,
Where are your Daddy Walsh's glasses?
Where are Gran's beads?
On her chair beside the fire.
The wireless, the races, the Grand National.
Bread and butter heaped with sugar
That fell onto the floor and crunched gorgeously under-
    foot.
The Men's Walk, the dock, evening,
the blind quay,
the slip, the steps the gunnel.

Beyond the Breakwater

Why did we all get big?
Why did Mir lose her curls?
There were no more prams
or little cardigans with white buttons.
Gran died. Daddy Walsh died.
Now Joe has slipped away.
We all grew up but their words are in my head today.
They echo back and forth.

7

Listening to the Hoover

The hum of a hoover being run over a carpet is one of my favourite sounds. It takes me back to days when I was kept home from school because of measles or a sore throat.

To make me feel better, I was usually put in my parents' bed and tucked up, the sheets straightened and the coverlet pulled up around my shoulders. I'd lie there, delighted to be on my own in the house with mother, who'd pop in and out through the morning to monitor my symptoms. Having her all to myself on a school morning when my father was gone to work and my sisters were off at school was a delicious treat that took the sting out of being sick.

I listened to the radio coming on downstairs and the floor being swept. I'd hear my mother taking the ashes out of the range and rummaging in a drawer. I'd listen to her running a tap to fill the kettle and putting it on the cooker to boil water for a hot water bottle for me. The novelty of listening to all those morning sounds was like being privy to my mother's secret world. I'd listen and wait for her to come back upstairs with the filled hot water bottle. She'd wrap it in something soft and put it down at my feet, asking me if I was feeling better.

'I think my throat is a bit better,' I'd croak, hoping she'd notice the ragged rasp of my voice.

Before she left, she'd tell me to open my mouth so she could look down at my tonsils. Then, straightening the bedclothes around me again, she'd put a cool hand on my forehead to feel if I was hot. 'I think you have a bit of a temperature all right. Lie down there now and try to sleep,' and before stepping out of the bedroom she'd look back to check that I was all right. I would remain prostrate in the bed, the picture of martyrdom, hoping she'd continue to run up and down to check on me.

If I had a temperature and my symptoms persisted, she would tell me she was going to get the doctor. Usually before his arrival, she'd do a bit of a tidy and hoover the bedroom. I'd lie there in state like Good Queen Bess, listening to her working, not wanting another thing in the world. Later, she would comb my hair and rub a damp cloth over my face in readiness for the doctor. She might put fresh pyjamas on me, specially aired and taken from the hot press.

I loved the hum of the hoover as she pushed the nozzle all around the edges of the room, under the dressing table and the bed, in behind the curtains and along by the wardrobe. I'd listen to her using it out on the landing by the stairs. When she was in the room or by the door, I'd have her in my sights and I'd breathe in deeply to fully enjoy the serenity of the moment. Sometimes, I'd drift in and out of sleep, the comforting sounds of Mama working lulling me into a state of deep contentment.

When Dr Coffey arrived downstairs, he would be ushered in with whispers and my ears would strain to hear what they were saying. 'The patient's in here, doctor,' I'd hear my mother say, recognising the hint of a smile in her voice.

There was a general holding of breath as we waited for him to discover the cause of my high temperature, itchy rash or swollen glands. Like a priest stepping up to the altar, time seemed to slow down when he was present and I'd watch his movements with intense interest. He'd walk in over the newly hoovered carpet, his very presence adding gravitas to the room. When he opened his impressively compact leather bag, the unfamiliar smell of antiseptic tweaked at my nose. He'd take his stethoscope out and listen to my breathing, moving the cold metal orb over my chest. 'Breathe in, and out, in and … out.' He'd put a spatula on my tongue. 'Say aaaah.' His movements, coupled with my responses, formed a kind of a choreographed dance and it seemed like the perfect coda to a morning with my mother.

Later, when my father came home for dinner, a bottle of Lucozade would appear on the bedside table. He might produce a bunch of grapes too. As these are given to invalids the world over, I'd nod weakly and smile, lying still in the bed.

Later in the week, when I was allowed down to the fire to join the others, I'd go down gingerly on legs that I was sure had wasted away after three whole days in bed, having read all about Clara in *Heidi* and Beth in *Little Women* taking similarly tentative steps during their convalescence. As a result, I'd allow my sisters to fuss over me and act as my slaves.

Soon, of course, I'd be back to normal and I'd be sent off to school, wrapped in extra layers. Like a released hostage, I'd go forth and brave the day; glad it was cold, as it was in keeping with my hard-pressed spirits. The biting breeze always helped me re-adjust to the harshness of life on the outside.

Then memories of my little holiday at home with my mother all to myself would gradually fade and I'd forget how the sound of the hoover humming away over the carpet had lulled me into a state of bliss and happy martyrdom. Until the next time, that is.

8

Saying Goodnight to Our Lady

We had a statue of Our Lady on the landing in our house in Lower Newtown when I was small. It was taller and heavier than I was at the time but I remember how, one night, my mother took it down for me so that I could inspect it properly. Then I had to say goodnight to her, and from that night on I used to say goodnight to Our Lady before I got into bed.

Her blue sash flowed down elegantly by her side and her hands were clasped together like a steeple, in prayer, coming up to just under her chin. Like her hands, her head seemed to be tilted slightly to one side as if she was listening intently to what I might whisper into her ear.

To me, she was like a giant-sized doll and I longed for the day when I might play with her and lie her down alongside me in the bed and roll her over and cuddle her. The next best thing was the chance I got each night to say goodnight to her before I got into bed. When I was ready for bed, as a treat, she'd be taken off the window sill where she sat on the return leading up to the attic, and I'd hug this plaster-cast image of the Blessed Virgin with all the intensity of my three or four years. I'd wrap my arms around her and lift her up off the attic stairs so that I could kiss her fervently on the cheeks. I remember the great weight of her. I could hardly lift her off the floor. It was difficult to get a good grip as she was slippery and the few points of purchase were all sharp, small edges, but regardless I'd struggle to lift her and carry her down a step or two where I'd talk to her and stroke her head.

There was a chip gone off her little nose but I didn't mind that. She had lovely rosy cheeks. Her skin was a matt pink. She had blue eyes and the most gentle and pleasing expression. I loved the smoothness of her blue folds down along her back, and the way her head and shoulders were so dry and rounded and cold to my touch.

I loved to run the flat of my hand down along the lines of her clothes, a well of love bubbling up in me. I remember the depth of my feelings for that statue. I never wanted to leave her. Although Our Lady was only made of plaster, she felt like a living, breathing presence to me.

'Now, I'll put her back on the ledge,' my mother would explain and pry me off the statue. 'She'll be all right there for the night. Go in to your bed now and I'll be in to say your prayers with you.' And I'd kiss Our Lady again and hug her one more time before relinquishing her to my mother. Then I'd go in to bed to say my prayers. 'And now I lay me down to sleep, I pray the Lord my soul to keep.'

I must have outgrown the statue or else I was weaned off the practice of saying goodnight to her, but I remember noticing her one night when I was a year or two older and feeling no bond with her at all or any need to say goodnight. The strong connection I'd felt had evaporated and all I saw was a mute statue on a sill. There was no throbbing presence emanating energy and love. It was just an ordinary statue again.

I looked and looked but I couldn't see or feel it. I was a bit nonplussed, but I knew it was gone. The little painted face was the same; the little hands like a steeple were still poised in prayer.

I longed for the angelic, childlike love I'd felt, but it had slipped away from me. The statue was a dead thing, even though I stood on the landing getting cold once or twice waiting in the hope that I'd feel it again.

9

Doing Alphonsus Road

On the morning of my Holy Communion, I was dressed in my new clothes: a white knee-length dress; a shoulder-length veil that was held in place with hairpins and an elastic band under my hair; new t-strap white shoes over turned-down ankle socks. I had gloves and a white cardigan with mother of pearl buttons. Everything crinkled when I moved.

I stepped gingerly over the hall tiles in the new shoes, rocking over the wooden lintel. I carried a handbag for my prayer book, my rosary beads and the 'handsels' I'd be getting later on of course – tokens of good luck that would mostly be in the form of money.

'Come here till I handsel you,' I'd hear as an admiring uncle or an aunt slipped a sixpence into my pocket with exaggerated discretion. 'Turn around now till I look at you.'

And so I made sure I went in to our neighbours next door to show them my finery on the day of my Holy Communion. I felt an obligation to parade my new outfit and visit as many neighbours as I could to collect whatever handsels they might like to offer. I felt like many first-born children: aware of my ability to give joy. I knew they'd be disappointed if they didn't get an opportunity to offer handsels and, as a result, I'd feel I had let them down if I didn't see them. So I left to knock on each door up along Lower Newtown. I went as far as the corner and turned up onto St Alphonsus Road.

I knocked and waited politely at the first door. When the door opened, I waited to hear the plaudits. Sensing the woman of the house was going to hansel me, I held out my white patent-leather bag with its tight metal clasp and passed it to her for the money. After receiving those handsels I went to the next house. This time I did notice a moment of uncertainty. My would-be benefactor turned to look over her shoulder, perhaps to her husband or an elderly parent within. When she peered out over my shoulder to see if I really was on my own, I began to wonder if perhaps it was time to return to home camp.

But my stash was growing so I continued up the hill.

I weighed the bag as I went. It was mostly shillings, half-crowns and sixpences. A pound or a ten-shilling note was a rarity. I would count it out carefully when I got home, I decided, in readiness for school the next day when the burning question amongst all us First Holy Communicants would be 'How much did you get?'

My mother, meanwhile, had come out to our gate, wondering where her angelic all-in-white daughter had gotten to. She looked up and down the road for a sight of me. She asked the Chesters who were playing on the wall across the road if they'd seen me. 'She's gone up to do Alphonsus Road,' one of them shouted.

My mother's heart must have sunk at the idea. Running in haste, she went to the corner and ran her eye up along the hill. When I heard her calling, I turned back happily and joined her at the corner. She took my hand and we rushed back to the house. As we went, I told her about the houses I had called to. I wasn't worried about her being cross at all. I imagined she'd be pleased with me because I knew I was a little angel in my dress.

Doing Alphonsus Road

She guided me in through the front door. When we were in the kitchen she recounted my exploits to my father. I saw them smiling but there was an element of embarrassment in their laughter too and I realised then that what I had done was not something I should repeat.

Annie Brophy

Not long after making my First Holy Communion, my mother took me and my sisters to Annie Brophy's photographic studio at 9 Barker Street in Waterford City. Brophy's experience of photographing all aspects of social, religious, sporting and educational life throughout the city and the county was second to none. Even to my young ears, the photographer was known to be legendary.

I was dressed in white from head to toe – dress, shoes, socks and gloves. I had my little white handbag draped over my arm and I took my veil along too. My two sisters were called in from the garden to be dressed in clean clothes and we all set off for the shoot.

My memory of the visit is dim but I do remember that it didn't take long, that Brophy was deft and brusque, completely focused on the job in hand. Her studio was a small room that was cool and quiet. A woman of few words, she pulled a brass tub closer to the stool where I was to sit. She moved my shoulders so that I was angled more towards her. The years have distilled my memory of the day. I remember how she arranged us: Miriam was put standing, while RoseAnn was asked to sit on a type of bench alongside our mother and me. Then Annie Brophy disappeared under the black cloth behind the tripod to drop the shutter and capture the image. All our energies became focused on that moment. She told me to look at her and not to move, and I waited to hear the click, terrified to move.

In the end, it was all about the photograph.

Brophy photographed me both sitting and standing, as well as taking the family shot of the four of us. My father was at work so he missed this occasion. In each photograph I am looking directly into the camera, smiling angelically. There is a kind of timelessness to these black-and-white photographs. I'm wearing my First Holy Communion medal and my two hands are together in my lap. Miriam's hair is tied back off her face with a great bow on the crown of her head. RoseAnn stares out cagily from under a silky fringe and a couple of ringlets hang down to the top of her shoulders. My mother looks like a film star in pearls and a sleeveless black and white dress. Brophy had photographed her almost thirty years earlier for her Holy Communion in the late 1930s. We treasure this photograph, as we have no other image of my mother as a child.

It was years later when I returned to Barker Street to retrace my steps. It's strange to walk in the footsteps of an icon. You sense a presence. At times, you imagine you are being taken by the hand and guided towards certain places. That's how it felt when RoseAnn and I were making a documentary about Annie Brophy, the great Waterford photographer, who left an archive of more than 65,000 negatives behind her.

Making the documentary, we became detectives, tiptoeing around our subject, trying to understand and discover what made her tick. From the photographs, it's clear to see that she loved symmetry. She liked pattern and balance in her pictures. Many of the pictures have the composition of a tableau about them and many have a stillness and a quietness to them. Yet there's truthfulness too. Fresh faces peer solemnly out at us from those earlier decades – serious, smiling, benign, vulnerable. They posed for her in the 1920s and 1930s before the war and afterwards, right up to the relative economic prosperity of the 1960s and 1970s.

She was a mould-breaker and a shrewd businesswoman. Brophy was only seventeen when she began her training as a young photographer in 1916. While still a schoolgirl at the Mercy Convent, she was singled out as being artistic and an excellent student, and sent to train at the successful Hughes photographic studio in Manor Street in Waterford. She served her time there until Mr Hughes moved to London. She set up her own studio in 1922, shortly after Mr Hughes left, and she did not retire until 1978.

'It was most unusual but it was well discussed at home with her parents,' Annie's niece, Carmel O'Regan, recalled. In the end, her family decided to support her in this endeavour.

Annie kept copies of everything she photographed for the simple reason that people often looked for copies, whether it was of wedding parties or missionaries, of ordinations or class groupings, and so everything was filed away. The negatives were kept at the top of the house, all stored in shirt or shoeboxes, in cigarette or biscuit boxes and whatever else was available. An entire bedroom was her filing cabinet.

Annie's day started in the morning at about 7 a.m. She rarely missed Mass. After that, she began her work in the studio. Later, she got the dinner for her and at least five other members of her family – two sisters, two married brothers who worked in the city and her youngest brother, Billy, who lived at home with the girls. Carmel told us that Annie was a highly organised individual.

Annie Brophy

The archive, which represents her continuous work over six decades, was kept together as a unit in Barker Street until she died in 1986. Today this photographic output stands as a testament to her creative talent and her steadfastness as an artist. It is kept in storage in Waterford's City Archive.

Carmel believes she projected her gentle, kind personality onto her sitters and that the photographs evoke Brophy's own character because there's 'a gentleness, a quietness, a perfection' in them. 'She loved people and she loved meeting people. She had a great sense of humour and had a very pleasant lifestyle without being ostentatious. It was a moderate life.' Carmel says her aunt liked an occasional flutter on the horses. She was always generous at Christmas time and always warm and kind.

Some days during our filming it felt as if Brophy was standing nearby, pointing us in certain directions. When we stood in front of her house, where she had lived all her life, we looked across at an old disused jail that had been used by the army during the Second World War to store turf. Tragically in 1943, after days of heavy rainfall, the foundations of the old wall became unsound and it fell heavily on the opposite row of houses, all 120 tonnes of turf. Nine people were killed as a result of the landslip. Annie Brophy would have known all the victims. It must have been a terrible scene that morning. Seventeen other people were injured, one of whom later died. But Brophy, the ultimate professional, had the determination and focus to take her camera and tripod outside to photograph the scenes.

On that March morning while filming the documentary, RoseAnn noticed a detail in the plaque on the wall that commemorates the tragedy. She called us over. Our cameraman Seamus Hayes, soundman Kieran Curtain and I stood in front of the jail wall. It took a moment for it to register – the incident had happened all those years ago on a Thursday, 4 March – and we happened to be standing on the very same spot, filming on a Thursday, 4 March.

A shiver rang down my back and I felt that the guiding hand of Annie Brophy was stronger than ever.

II

Tall as a Mountain was He

Sitting tight as a ball in the rattan chair, deep in the gloam of the dining room, I'd watch the story of Daniel Boone unfold on the small television. 'With an eye like an eagle and as tall as a mountain was he,' the theme song declared.

I remember how in one episode of *Daniel Boone*, the eponymous pioneering hunter and woodsman of the early American frontier was tracking hunters through a fearsome canyon. The moon was full and danger lurked around each rock. There were whistles and shrieks at every step. The tension ratcheted up as Boone didn't realise he was being stalked by a black panther, crouched on a rock overhead.

At the very second when the cat was about to pounce, my father crept in behind me, gripped my shoulders and shouted, 'Watch out!'

My heart nearly stopped. I whirled around and berated my own dear Papa, crying tears of terror and relief.

I loved being lost in make-believe; I loved wandering the mountains with the rippin'est, roarin'est, fightin'est man the frontier ever knew!

At that age, we slipped easily from states of extreme excitement into terror. We lived in fear of 'the Bogeyman', knowing that he would catch us if we didn't get into bed and go to sleep quickly. He was behind the door in the dark. He was outside in the yard or in the scullery at night waiting in the corner ready to pounce on us.

In my eyes, Gingee Jones, an old man who sometimes shuffled past our house, seemed to fit the bill of the Bogeyman. When he appeared, I'd run for my life, fright propelling me along the street or into the house. The poor man most likely only wandered the streets of our city looking to pick up work, but the mere hint of his emergence on the horizon was enough to send me racing.

Sometimes if he passed when we were all out skipping, the neighbouring children and I would stop and crane our necks for a look. He wore a dirty coat that was full of holes and held together with safety pins. He pushed an old pram. Maybe he was a rag and bone man, who made a living by going from street to street, collecting unwanted items from houses along the way so that he could sell them on. Sometimes it felt as if we wished him there because the terror of his passing sent such a thrilling shiver down our backs and into our hearts. When, spectre-like, he'd move off down the hill, it was as if he'd just risen jangling and fierce from an old rusty bed. In the distance, to us on the footpath, he seemed to leave a silence in his wake. As he wandered off out of our sights, we'd remain quiet, peering around the corner to catch one last sight of him.

Now in adulthood, I try to remember those forgotten times of waiting for the Bogeyman and watching Daniel Boone on television. It was a time when we called any kissing or romantic stuff seen on the television 'darling business'. If we saw the heads of actors coming together in readiness for a steamy kiss, we'd exclaim: 'Oh no, darling business!' thereby alerting each other to the horrors about to unfold on the screen. We'd all turn away in disgust and squirm in our seats, hiding behind our fingers until it was over or – if it continued for too long – we'd run out of the room altogether. These exhibitions of amorous arousal caused us such exquisite embarrassment.

Looking back, I also reach for glimpses of the mornings when the tinkling sound of my mother going to the drawer to get a bottle opener was like a beckoning bell. The sound of her opening her small bottle of Guinness, which she took to build herself up following years of illness with tuberculosis, would bring the three of us running up like goslings wanting a sup from her glass. We'd gather, our hands on her lap, waiting until she passed the glass to each of us for one long glorious mouthful of the black yeasty stuff. We'd smack our lips at the satisfaction of our voyage-long drought being slaked.

I reach for the sound of my father massaging tobacco in the heel of his palm, pressing it fine with a ritualistic motion, and the sound of the spittle he'd create in the bowl of the pipe when the crackling and popping sounded. This always marked the end of the day for us.

I reach for the soft sound of his hand along a piece of board as he wrote out the alphabet with a marker to teach me my letters before I went to school. I watch him write, crouching at my side, handsome, eager, transmitting that energy to me. Like Daniel Boone, with an eye like an eagle and as tall as a mountain was he.

12

Nuns

Nuns populated my early school days in Waterford city. During my time living on Lower Newtown I attended St John of God National School. Lay teachers were few and far between, but nuns swept by me every day. They were ever-present in that pale speckle-tiled primary school of the mid-1960s, rustling at the top of the classroom in front of the blackboard, swirling round like great battleships ready to swoop down on any wrong-doer. They walked in black habits along cool corridors, beads and keys rattling and slapping against each other. They were always busy, regal, elegantly bustling. We pulled back out of their way, fearfully, instinctively, the polished sheen of that specially made half-inch-thick stick or 'bata' never too far from our minds.

Nuns all smelled the same. When a nun in her gabardine rigging came up close in a classroom, the smell of the cloth, imbued with a rich mix of soap, starch, sweat, camphor balls, polish, incense and old refectory aromas, was overpowering. But a nun rarely came too near except on occasion in class when she might show you how to write an 'r' or a 'q'. Then this personage would squeeze into the seat beside you and, taking your pen, demonstrate in best copperplate how to achieve the great curved letters.

The pungent odour of that cloaked body mingling perhaps with a bouquet of fumes from her hidden undergarments could enclose and momentarily suffocate you. It could leave you dumb-founded, unable to answer even the simplest question.

Nuns

'How do you spell this, Catherine?' she might ask in crystal clear, rurally accented syllables. Or, 'Isn't that right, Catherine?' And the class would wait, while I, sitting in mystification, the colour rising up my cheeks, could only mumble, 'Yes, sister', smile and wait until she'd moved away. To be so near this musty-scented nun, who could wield a disciplinary thwack with great vigour, or wedge a pointed finger in between your shoulder blades, or firmly catch hold of your arm and propel you vigorously into a classroom, was more potent than the smell of chocolate or even cod liver oil.

Seeing a nun up close was a truly fascinating and horrifying moment. With no hair visible except for an occasional facial sprout, the pasty-toned skin was a lunar landscape of mystery to us pupils. And I remember their complex, unreadable expressions, hinting at the private world they inhabited where women watched and counted, coveted and conspired, prayed and purloined to attain holiness and sanctity. They were worlds away, cloistered from the play areas where we skipped and ran.

On our rare visits to the convent we were provided with a chance to peep into their world of polished surfaces, where reverberating bells and rushing skirts, stony-faced statues and hollow, scarifying whispers occupied wide corridors and stairways. The sound of their beads striking their keys made little irregular clicks that sounded like beetles when they moved.

In class we pasted pictures of leaves, trees, doors, cows and thrushes into our copybooks. Using fat brushes dipped into jam jars, we painted globs of gloopy paste onto stiff paper.

As I progressed through school, we learned to knit socks and gloves, to embroider tablemats and cushion covers and to sew hems and buttonholes, collars and pockets. We learned about

Fionn Mac Cumhaill and the Tuatha Dé Danann, about the Bronze Age and the Iron Age, and about the rivers, mountains and towns of Ireland.

We learned to walk in a procession and to file quietly into the assembly hall. We learned to pray and to rise or sit at our desks at the barest nod or look of command. We were told by the nuns how to sit, how to walk into a room, how to stand.

One day in school, each of us shivered when word went round that a nun had died. She was to be waked in the convent that night. The thought of her lying on a table, icy cold to the touch, was palpable. Her ghostly presence fell on darkened cubicles like the shadow of a great bird of prey. We imagined her lying in the convent chapel, her body prostrate, rosary beads entwined around her fingers, her yellow skin sleek and shiny in death. She had us cowering in dimly lit stairwells, terrified we'd see her face in front of us.

All through school, nuns remained a source of mystery and ridicule, reverence and revulsion. They were curiosities, not women, not mothers, not aunts but strange, mysterious, medieval beings that were never seen to bathe or undress or shake out their hair. In ages past, they'd been walled up in towers or convents never to emerge. Were these teaching nuns an offshoot, an aberration that strode into our classrooms to direct our eyes?

Today, I wonder about nuns and how they were once omnipresent in our lives. I wonder where they have all gone and if they were just misunderstood. Might they actually have been benign beings, or were they really scary?

13

Jackie Kennedy in Woodstown

I was eight years old when we came up from the strand in Woodstown one day in our sandals and swimsuits to catch a glimpse of Jackie Kennedy with her entourage as they rode by. We waited by the side of that country road, alongside other small groups of day-trippers, all dotted along the verge, standing patiently in the sun in the hope of seeing her. Perhaps my father's absence added a certain sense of expectancy, of being light and lost.

It was during the summer holidays, when my mother used to drive us as children out to Woodstown to spend the day on the strand. She'd pack sandwiches and a flask and take a blanket, towels and our swimsuits. She'd park the little green Mini near the Saratoga Bar and down we'd go onto the beach to spend the day splashing away, light and easy in the breeze, until my father came to join us in the evening, jumping on a bus after work to catch the last couple of rays of sun and a swim before we all headed home to our house in the city.

The strand of fine sand and cockleshells in Woodstown, County Waterford is golden, a wide expanse stretching along the riverbank. The water at the mouth of the Suir estuary was always shallow, warm and sparkling. All those days were filled with buckets and shovels, cockle-picking and splashing. We'd flounce in and out of the waves, our swimsuit frills trickling tiny cascades of water down over our spindle-shank legs.

While we waited to see Jackie Kennedy that day, my mother held my sisters' hands in case they'd run out under a car. The sun beat down and the sand was hot underfoot, spilling in loose, golden grains onto the tar of the road all along the way. A man with a hailer passed along and warned everyone to keep back. He moved along briskly, having a friendly word here and there with some of the women further along the line, who were also waiting with their children. I jumped up and down, thrilled at the thought of seeing Jackie Kennedy. It was clear from the way the crowd was talking that she was the essence of glamour and fairytale romance.

'Watch out for her now,' my mother told us. 'She'll be along any minute.'

I especially remember how it felt to be standing there, excited, expectant and warmed by the communal buzz of affection for Jackie and her two children: Caroline, who was nine, and John John, who was six. My heart went out to them when I learned they'd lost their father.

The air seemed to tingle that day in 1967 as we waited to see her. There was a distinct touch of stardust in the air as we stood beside my mother to see the beautiful young widow who'd been marked by tragedy. The fizz of heat added greatly to the power of the moment. Our wait seemed endless until finally someone shouted, 'Look, she's coming,' and the thrill of her arrival went through us. All heads peered down the road to catch a glimpse of her. Suddenly the place was full of the sound of horses' hooves cantering over the stones.

'Keep back, they're coming close,' my mother said, pulling us in. 'Do you see her?' she asked us. I looked, but the adults all around me combined with the gentle jostling that her arrival had caused, left me disorientated and confused.

Jackie Kennedy in Woodstown

But there she was – one of the party, a slim woman, erect, her back tilting forward slightly as she trotted by on a dark horse. Had there been the flash of a smile? I couldn't be sure. I waved but she passed like a streak across our day and it's all a jumble now. I remember them trotting by in an explosion of noise down along the road, turning in at the main entrance gates of Woodstown House, across the road and down from the Saratoga.

Within seconds the clamour of the riders had faded and they were gone.

A general sigh of sated pleasure washed over us as we walked back along the path towards the steps down to the strand and our belongings. The day seemed different, as if the sun had gone behind a cloud. The sand was cold and we stood, shivering, pulling on our cardigans, anxious to see our father, watching out in case he would not come.

The dangers of not having him arrive now suddenly snapped at my heels. As I tried to fasten my buttons, I kept watch, checking to see him walk along so that he could greet us and bring us in for one last swim. And suddenly there he was.

14

The River Suir Runs Through It

The bridge across the River Suir was once the main link between Waterford and the residents of Ferrybank on the other side. For those who lived in the village of Ferrybank, especially in the 1930s and 1940s when my father was growing up, all aspects of city life were on offer on the opposite side of the river.

He and his brothers and sisters knew their bridge then as Redmond Bridge, an elegant Victorian-style construction that was opened in 1913. It would be over eighty years before this stylish bridge became unsafe and had to be replaced by a new concrete bridge known as Rice Bridge.

My father was a teenager in the late 1930s. He knew that Ferrybank stretch of river as well as anyone. His mother did all her shopping for the family in the city. He'd often seen her heading off, shopping bag hanging over her arm, as she aimed to buy shoes or a coat for one of them. He was one of twelve, so there was a constant flow of movement by her over and back to the city.

Mitching from school one day and looking for somewhere to pass the time, my father ducked into the Dominican Church on the city side of the bridge. While he was kneeling at the altar rails, no doubt in contemplation of his sins as a reluctant student, he heard the patter of tiny heels coming up the aisle. Something familiar about the sound made him turn just in time to see his mother genuflect and kneel beside him. He slipped away in double-quick time, leaving her to say a prayer before continuing on her way into the city to do her shopping.

In the 1930s my father and the other Foley brothers used to get a ferry across the river on their way to secondary school in the city, as the distance was shorter and the boat trip was more exciting than the bridge. They were taken across in big open rowing boats, each crewed by two men. The cost of a weekly ticket was three old pence.

'All the moods of that great Waterford river were known to us,' my father's brother, Donal, wrote in his autobiography, *Three Villages*. 'The waves could be near mountainous on the day when the river would be swept with an easterly breeze. During the late spring and all through summer,' he continues, 'it was an idyllic experience to cross that great expanse of dark green water as it lapped the quays, and looked south to the lush tree-lined banks, Cromwell's Rock and Fitzgerald's Island.'

Later, in the 1950s, my father worked in the railway station that is located on the Ferrybank side of the bridge. There, in its heyday, over 700 people were employed. Waterford had an allocation of fifty-three locomotives with lines running to Cork, Limerick, Dublin, New Ross and Rosslare. In excess of 500 wagons were handled each day in the large fan-shaped goods yard that was situated between Mount Misery and the river.

Of an evening, my father would cycle from Ferrybank across the bridge to meet my mother on Meagher's Quay in the city. Sparkling with vitality, he would race across, cycling over the river, on the mode of transport favoured by young men at the time, pushing against the traction of the bike's thin rubber tyres on the tarred surface of the bridge. He must have been handsome and fresh like new-mown hay – stick-thin and all teeth, with a sharply drawn jaw, a brilliant smile and the creamy skin of a country-grown boy. He wore his hair short, oiled back with Brylcreem, and his wide trouser legs were kept tightly in place with bicycle clips.

Traffic was light in those days. There were gentle ambient sounds: no electronic beeping or telephonic voices punctuated the air, only the bellowing of animals on the way to the mart and the screeching of trains into the station.

It's over 100 years now since the once-new bridge to span the river was nearing completion. The noise of pounding and hammering could be heard all along the quays as the great ferro-concrete edifice, the Redmond Bridge, was erected. It was completed in February 1913, at a total cost of £71,000. As it was named in his honour, Mr John Redmond MP, leader of the Irish Parliamentary Party, opened it.

The day was a perfect occasion, according to local reports, apart from a 'suffragette incident', which an editorial in the *Munster Express* says caused a bit of a stir. It seems friends were welcoming Mr Redmond at the station, after his arrival from Dublin, when he was accosted by two ladies who alighted from the third-class carriage of the same train. One of them, said to be a Dublin woman, pushed her way towards him and said, 'You are going to open a free bridge are you? Will you open a free bridge to votes for women?' Mr Redmond just smiled, the newspaper reported. Local writer and retired train driver Jack O'Neill recalls this and many other forgotten incidents in his book, *Waterford Through the Lens of Time*.

But the history of this bridge goes back even further, as the

Redmond Bridge was not, in fact, the original bridge. Its first incarnation was built in 1793 and was named as The Timber Bridge, though it was known locally as 'Timber Toes'.

It operated as a toll bridge for over 100 years. In those days a coach and six horses cost three shillings to pass, a pedestrian with baggage was a penny, a pedestrian without baggage paid a half penny, twenty cattle was three shillings and, most telling of all, for all the mourners following a coffin at a funeral there was no charge. Perhaps this most of all captures the spirit of the people who lived along the Suir.

15

Geneva Barracks

I have a black and white photograph of myself as a child with my mother kneeling in the grass beside me, smiling. We are at Geneva Barracks in Passage East at a summer fair that was held there. I am dressed as Little Red Riding Hood – in a kind of djellaba down to my sandalled feet. I have a basket on my arm but my tear-stained face shows what an unwilling participant I was in the fancy dress of the early 1960s. I can remember being afraid because I thought I was going to meet the wolf. But tear-stained or not, I came away with first prize in that year's fancy dress competition.

A few years later, my mother dressed my sister Miriam and I as Gabby and Statia, two aul' ones from *Tolka Row*, RTÉ's first soap opera about a community living on Dublin's northside. Again my mother entered us into the fancy dress at Geneva Barracks. The two of us held hands as we paraded round the ring in our long dresses and little jaunty hats, the netting pulled forward to give that extra touch of verisimilitude. We jostled with the other contestants, all of us with cardboard signs hanging from our necks on strings declaring what characters we were supposed to be.

I have photographs of those times when we posed in the lee of the derelict Geneva Barracks – my mother, my grandfather, my father, my sisters and me – different years, different photographs. I remember the swinging cots, the sandwiches and the cups of strong tea from wobbly tables in the field. I remember walking through the overgrown field, my father having to lift us over thistles and cow-dung. I remember in particular how we paraded around the ring in Geneva Barracks and the view of the Suir as it flowed down past Crooke and Duncannon, spreading out beneath us on the other side towards Hook Head and out to sea.

Geneva Barracks was a settlement that was turned into a military barracks in the eighteenth century, following a decision by the group of Swiss settlers it was intended for not to live there. They'd been invited to come by Ireland's governing Protestant Ascendancy, who had a plan to establish a colony of intellectuals and artists in the area. The idea was that this group of skilled people from Geneva would settle in Passage East. The site was acquired in 1783 and the renowned architect James Gandon was commissioned to design a series of buildings that would look out over the Waterford estuary. But the arrangement fell through and the Irish parliament instead decided to use the site as a military base. Soon the soldiers were installed and in time the barracks became a frightening and cruel holding centre, an internment camp. This is how it became the resting place of the Croppy Boy.

'At Geneva Barracks that young man died,' my mother used to sing. Even though the song was a dirge-like lament, we loved all ten verses of it and we'd slip easily into a kind of drowsy trance when my mother, who was a proud Passage woman, sang about the Croppy Boy. It was her party piece and though she was not a confident singer, none of us could resist the powerful and poignant pull of that song and the way she sang it with such grace and honesty.

My mother usually sang this 1798 song at Christmas-time.

A hush would fall on us when, after some coaxing, her timid tremolo would steal out across the room and we'd be hooked.

> *Good men and true in this house who dwell*
> *To a stranger buachaill I pray you tell*
> *Is the Priest at home or may he be seen*
> *I would speak a word with Father Green.*

Her version is the one that was written by County Down man, William B. McBurney, who used the pseudonym Carroll Malone. It first appeared in 1845 in *The Nation*, the weekly nationalist newspaper. It tells the story of a young man who stops in a church on his way to fight in the 1798 rebellion. He goes into the confessional, to a cloaked figure, and kneels for the penitential rite. But the figure is a British soldier in disguise, a wolf in priest's clothes. After the youth has completed his confession, the soldier reveals himself and proceeds to arrest the young man and take him to prison. The boy is later executed in Geneva Barracks.

We thoroughly enjoyed those sing-songs, but there comes a time in life when the make-up of family get-togethers changes and so it happened with us. Once we'd left the 1970s behind us occasions to sing dwindled and after 1980 I don't recall my mother ever singing 'The Croppy Boy' again.

Some sing 'The Parting Glass', others sing 'I Did It My Way', but when we gathered around my mother's grave just a handful of years ago, there was only one song my sisters and I could bring ourselves to sing. Miriam picked it out on the fiddle and we followed her. The pathos of those notes was never so heartbreaking. Today when I look at those old Geneva Barracks photographs from the 1960s, all I see is my mother's beauty.

16

Feeding the Birds

When you are small, it is difficult to stand still for a long time in the middle of a wintry garden. Tiny rustles carry in the frosty air, little rivulets of water gurgle down the path and ice cracks down at your toes.

It is a fairly existential state, suspended in time, standing up-right between frozen beds, holding breadcrumbs in your hands, arms stretched heavenwards, your fingers splayed, waiting for a 'willie' wagtail or a thrush to alight. I knew if I wobbled in any way I'd frighten the birds away.

Children are fascinated by all the sounds and movements around them. Heaven was in those moments when I listened to the surf of time, my conscious mind teetering on that precipice between expectation and imminent realisation, caught between those two states of being – of remaining still so that I could hear it all correctly and understand.

It seemed an eternity passed while I waited in anticipation for those elusive birds to land. I do remember the howling under-tow of failure lapping at the edges of my dream, the constant presence of aviary rejection. The idea that an occasional bird, a hungry chaffinch or a sparrow, might fly low after the frost and rest on my hand, or my head, or on the discarded terracotta chimney pot I'd used to create a little additional nest with twigs, was so appealing that I sometimes held my breath.

In order to balance, I often had to vary my stance, especially if I was trying to stand on one leg in the hope that the birds would think I was a bare leafless tree. But that was harder, especially as the dog was a distraction when he bounded up the garden steps and tried to jump on me. The cat usually stayed on the windowsill, not interested in anything outside of her own feline sphere.

There was a little robin, red-breasted against the cold sky, which hopped down close. I saw her little jerky head pinning me with her beady eye from a perch on our gutter. She watched me with an amused cockiness that caused my hand to shake and my eyes to feel as if they were about to come out on sticks as I tried to remain stock-still. She was quite near but too clever by far to come any closer. When the cat moved slowly across the top of the wall, she flew off like a blithe spirit, light and ephemeral.

I heard my mother in the kitchen opening drawers, peeling potatoes, her syncopated movements a steady backdrop to my dance of stillness outside in the sleeping garden.

'Don't sit on those wet steps or you'll get a cold up through your kidneys,' she shouted.

'No, Mama, I won't,' I shouted down, hoping my voice would not frighten the birds away and undo all the trust I had built up. Our garden was bordered on each side by tall laurel hedges. In winter, when the sun was low in the sky, it seemed long and narrow like a railway track, sparkling and raw in the frosty light.

I can't remember what my inspiration was for this act. Did I hear Julie Andrews singing 'Feed the Birds' on the radio, or perhaps I'd seen a painting of St Francis of Assisi, the patron saint of animals, in one of our books, the *Lives of the Saints*? I had seen my mother putting bread out for the birds but maybe it was Snow White I'd read about. Whatever my inspiration, it was a feat to remain so stationary under the sky in all its opaque cloudiness miles above.

Once the cold or tiredness became too much I'd return to the house. Inside, the howling of the wind when it blew under the dining room door held me enthralled, listening to the *whuuuoooo* as the breeze sang under the door. *Whuuuooooooo* it went, rising again to a cry before dying away.

I bent down close to the gap where the breeze was, between the saddle and the door, and listened to its music. It rose like an oboe in a minor key, leading an orchestra of sounds: the crackle of the fire in the grate, the rattle of the letter box and the creak of the kitchen door, all playing together.

I had to listen carefully to their secret conversation. *Whuu-uooooo*, sang the wind, reaching a pitch like a tornado, and then it came under the door like an exhalation, and died away and there was quiet, and I stayed still on my belly, my ear to the crack, waiting for it to blow again under the door, listening to its dying cry, and I wondered what it was saying to the house.

And there I lay, suspended in a nether world of darkness and fire, of ice and cold, the world of winter, loving the wind and its whispering sigh – until the next day, recharged, I would once again race out to the back garden and attempt to coax the birds to feed from my outstretched hands.

17

Newfoundland

The cold breeze that blows along the quays in Waterford city is legendary. It whips around Reginald's Tower and gathers speed up along the river, taking no prisoners. Shoppers don't dawdle. They rush along from the bridge to Kelly's, carrying bags, their heads down to protect against the bitter cold. You'll hear 'Twould cut you like a knife', or 'Twould skin a brass monkey today'.

It was the same in the early 1530s when the first ship sailed out from Waterford through the estuary to voyage across the Atlantic to Newfoundland in search of cod. Over the coming centuries, these strong winds were to guide hundreds of ships to the fishing grounds on the other side of the world. In time, at least half a million young men would leave the quays of Waterford to go to Newfoundland in North America to fish. I never knew this when I was at school in Waterford.

In its heyday Waterford Port was one of the world's busiest centres of trade and commerce in Europe. The Vikings were the first to discover the harbour's excellent sheltered conditions. At high tide there was fifty feet of deep water in the river and you could sail fifty miles upstream.

At the height of the cod trading industry, from the mid-1700s up to 1830, there were 200 sailing ships leaving the quays of Waterford each year, bound for Newfoundland. What a sight it must have been! They carried between 4,000 and 8,000 young men on board, all on contract to the city's merchants. They usually went to fish off Newfoundland for a minimum of eight months. The clatter and ringing of schooners is palpable still in the air, only muted by time.

According to Jack Burtchaell, a local historian who brings visitors on daily walking tours through Waterford city, the men who manned the cod boats generally went away for periods of up to twenty months. Before they left, the fleet was stocked with food, ropes, tack, clothes and all the other provisions needed for such protracted voyages. It was all brought on board along the waterfront in Waterford. The chandlers and merchants made a fortune. Then the ships would sail down the estuary some six or seven miles and moor off Passage East. They'd wait there for the river pilot and until the tides and winds were favourable, and then set off. It's easy to imagine the sight today, as I stand on the Blind Quay in Passage East. The choppy white waters still run by the Spit Light Beacon, washing up against the breakwater and lashing the fishing vessels that plough the river.

How did they manage the hunger and the cold, the chilblains and the wet during those months of fishing in icy waters? The cod, some as long and thick as a man's leg, were split and dried on timber flakes. Salted cod with a shelf-life of twenty years was the most easily transported form of protein in those pre-refrigeration years, being flat and hard as wood. While the fishing and salting was in progress, the men entertained themselves on the frozen waters of Newfoundland by playing hurling and by faction fighting – 'on an inter-county basis', says Burtchaell with a twinkle in his eye. County and parochial rivalry was fierce in those distant days – it still is – and hurling, in particular, is a great and passionate sport. The fishermen who manned the fleets came from some of the great hurling counties – Waterford, Kilkenny, Tipperary and Wexford. The men from Wexford, also known as 'Yellow Bellies', used to meet on a certain street corner in the town of St John's in Newfoundland. It's known today as Yellow Belly Corner.

Some argue that it was the crews of the cod fishing fleets playing hurling on the ice throughout the winter, which, in time, gave rise to one of Canada's most popular sports, ice hockey. Burtchaell points out that in Irish the word for giving the ball a wallop is *poc*, the word now used to describe the puck in hockey.

Waterford fishermen and mariners found much-needed employment in Newfoundland. Up to 35,000 people, drawn overwhelmingly from Waterford and its hinterland, settled in Newfoundland between 1800 and 1830. The first three Newfoundland bishops came from the Waterford area.

Before the ships returned home to Waterford, the cod was salted and traded all over the world, from the Baltic Sea to Brazil, with the ships bringing goods back from these distant countries in turn. Then, when the men returned, 'they'd hit the town like a hurricane. It was Mardi Gras (after nearly two years away) for two months,' Burtchaell explains, relishing the idea. 'They were broke by the third,' he adds.

This boom industry fuelled a building boom in Waterford. New houses owned by the wealthy merchant families were built. Roads were improved and the cultural and social life of the city developed.

But by the mid-1800s, the fishing boom had begun to peter out and the market for cod, which had made wealthy men of the ship-owning merchants – the Fogartys, the Mullowneys, the Farrells, the Wyses, the Cashins and the Rices – had dried up.

Newfoundland

I wander into the Granville Hotel on the quay in Waterford. It's still one of the oldest and most elegant establishments in the city. The building was built by the Newports, one of the city's well-known merchant families. Thomas Meagher, whose family had emigrated to Newfoundland from south Tipperary in the late 1700s, returned home in 1819 and bought the house. His son, the patriot and soldier Thomas Francis Meagher, who grew up to become the famous Young Irelander, a decorated hero of the American Civil War and who was acting governor of Montana when he died in 1867, was born in this house in 1823. It was sold in 1825 to Charles Bianconi, the father of public transport in Ireland, who first established a hotel here.

Burtchaell smiles as he recalls some of the people he has met in Newfoundland on his many visits – John Mannion, Professor of Geography at the Memorial University of Newfoundland, who was honoured at NUI Galway for his pioneering research into the historic area; the Porters, who came from Kilmacow and went to Newfoundland; and the octogenarian Ally O'Brien, who speaks and sounds as if he was 'straight out of south Kilkenny. His people left in 1815. You'd swear he was from Ballyhale. It's like a step back in time to visit his kitchen,' says Burtchaell. 'The range on one side, the Pope on the other.'

As I walk the grey cobbled streets, passing the Catholic Cathedral of the Most Holy Trinity – built on Barronstrand Street between 1793 and 1796 with money made in Newfoundland – I feel a strong connection with the past. Grey stones tell no lies. Designed by architect John Roberts, it's easy to feel the centuries slip away. Inside, Waterford Crystal chandeliers light its ancient baroque interior. A plaque on the wall commemorates Bishop James Louis O'Donel OSF, who was born in 1737 in Knocklofty, Co. Tipperary. He was appointed the first Apostolic Vicar and Bishop of Newfoundland in 1796.

Talamh an Éisc is the Irish for Newfoundland, which literally translates as 'the land of the fish'. That phrase has the ring of truth about it. Talamh an Éisc meant money, prosperity, adventure and camaraderie to the men who sailed out of Waterford harbour.

The quays of Waterford today are soaked in sunshine. A millennium sculpture in William Vincent Wallace Plaza on the riverfront, inspired by the Viking ships, is where young men now skateboard. Its white lines shimmer in the light. If you listen carefully you can almost hear the rigging of hundreds of ships jiggling in the breeze.

Ring

Moving

The road to Ring was long and winding. It was August 1970 and the sun shone all through the day we left Waterford city and went to live in the Gaeltacht far away. It was only forty miles or so along the coast, but to us, sitting in the back of the Mini – now a newer red version – we may as well have been going to live in Tasmania.

We sat with our arms around Jingle, our black and white mongrel Jack Russell terrier. Like any good dog he sat panting beside us, waiting for the next episode of his life to begin. In some ways he seemed to embody our curiosity and watchfulness.

Leaving the neighbours, the house, the garden and the road was a wrench for my mother, who cried all the way to the Holy Cross pub in Butlerstown. My father was more stoical but underneath his bluster we could see that he was equally tense and upset, so he pulled in to the Holy Cross for us to have a drink and compose ourselves. There were minerals for us, while half measures of spirits helped revive our parents.

We were on the road again in no time, going through the Sweep and Kilmeaden, on towards Kilmacthomas and Lemybrien, Tarr's Bridge and then Dungarvan, where my father pulled into Grattan Square and we surveyed our new local town. Miriam noted the shops and their signs. Having just learned about punctuation at school she read out exactly what she saw. 'J Dot Mountain,' she declared, reading the grocery shop's front sign with all the authority and perspicacity of her nine years. She proceeded to read the other shop fronts too: Lawn's Bookmakers, Hill's Chemist. There were shops owned by Currans, Fields and Greenes. We laughed at the strange surnames and scrutinised the square for more examples. Mama and Dada laughed with us. 'J Dot Mountain,' my father said, grinning, and we were all giggling in no time.

Soon we were on the way again, turning off the main Cork to Waterford road to drive out along the length of the Ring peninsula. It was a narrow, winding road. It wove its way under a tunnel of trees that formed a canopy of leaves overhead. We followed its meandering way, curving around bends, my father nearly slowing the car to a halt as he went carefully around two sharp hairpin bends. The hanging ivy that fell like a fringe over the second hairpin bend, Droichead an Uisce, seemed like a gateway. The ivy was dark and damp, glistening and dripping. We went on, shivering as we passed through the cool shadows. We three girls in the back seat followed each twist and turn with growing interest. It felt as if we were entering a magical place deep under the trees.

When we arrived at the top of Robert's Cross, a wide expanse of road opened out under a great dome of sky that stretched above us. We pulled in so that we could take a look at the view – the bay beneath us and the great sky overhead. Wisps of cloud floated in the blue air. The bay rippled under the hot August sun. Across the water, the Comeragh Mountains with the Knockmealdowns off to the west formed a great backdrop to the town of Dungarvan and to the east we saw the coastline of Waterford disappearing into the distance like a pencil line towards Stradbally, Ballyvoyle, Bonmahon and a spot at the furthest point that was the Hook lighthouse. The road in front led along the spine of the peninsula of Ring itself, which spread out before us like a great green blanket, lying on a high bumpy bed with the blue sea tucked in snugly all along its sides. The furthest promontory, Helvick Head, could be seen way off in the distance. Close to the land we could also see a couple of boats just beyond Helvick Pier.

We drove on down the hill towards the lower fields and boreens of An Rinn. When we pulled in to Baile na nGall, it seemed as if the neighbours at the top of the village had been waiting for our arrival. The sun shone and those at their gates along a line of cottages below us waved shyly. Others stood on the opposite side of the road to watch the arrival. One or two called a greeting to my father in Irish. 'Tá fáilte rómhaibh, Joe.' He walked over to say hello to these friends from his childhood. Among those who lived close by were contemporaries of his such as Larry Kenneally, Tomás Breathnach, John Paul, Micil Tóibín and Willy Hally. They would now be our neighbours.

The house was a source of great mystery. It was set well back from the road, a tall, upright, two-storey building. Inside, we raced up the steep staircase to explore. On the landing there was a door going left and another one going to the right. We chose the right door and found ourselves in one large bedroom. A door from this led directly into another room. From this we saw another door and this we discovered led into a third bedroom and from that room, there was another door leading to a final bedroom. We flew through these four linked rooms, exclaiming as if we had discovered a box of tricks. Jingle followed us, adding his tuppence-worth to the noise. The rooms had skylights, so we climbed up on whatever we could to open these interesting outlets to the roof, hoisting up the old iron bars that slotted into secure pegs, and from our vantage point we looked out onto the road, the fuchsia hedge, the sky and the fields beyond.

One of my first expeditions in Baile na nGall was up to Harty's farm, which was only a stone's throw away from us, to get the milk. Up the hill I went with the empty canteen, going over tarred stones where great plops of cow dung were drying in the sun. As I neared the opening into Harty's yard, I picked my way carefully through the still steaming, dark-green pools of pungent dung. Flies clung to this gloopy stuff that was still running and settling between the stones.

Cows were mooing in the field behind me and I saw Seán Harty walking there in amongst his herd. I went up to the door of the thatched house and knocked, and his mother, Mrs Nóiní Harty, was inside.

'Tar isteach,' she called. A great white enamel bucket of milk stood on the table covered with a tea towel. She stood up slowly and with effort to take my can and scoop milk out of the bucket with a ladle into my small gallon.

'Cathain a tháinig sibh?' she asked me. *When did ye arrive?*

'Inniu,' I told her in my smattering of Irish. *Today.*

'Conas atá d'athair is do mháthair?' she asked. *How are your father and your mother keeping?*

'Tá siad go maith, go raibh maith agat.' *They are good, thank you.*

Time passed in the quiet there as I stood in my dream world watching her pour the milk in one long white rush of liquid into my gallon.

'Tá sé go deas inniu,' I said. *It is nice today.*

'Tá, tá sé an-bhrothallach,' she said, referring to the great heat in the day. *Yes, it is very hot.*

Over the coming weeks, we met lots of new people. I was soon using phrases that Mrs Harty had used to me. 'Tá sé an-bhrothallach,' I said to a passing neighbour. 'Ta sé an-mheirbh ar fad,' he answered. 'An-mheirbh,' I'd say to myself, storing that one away too. *Very muggy.*

We were soon going down to the strand to pick periwinkles with all the others and selling them to the dealer on the fish lorry at the end of the week. There was great competition to find the best beds of seaweed where you'd find the greatest amounts of hidden winkles. It was cold, wet work but we had great sport and we could earn a few pounds.

Sometimes, we walked to Helvick to stand on the pier and watch the fishermen throwing their boxes of fish up onto the quay right at our feet. 'Seachain do chosa, a chailín,' they'd shout – *watch your feet, girl* – warning me to stand back.

Then it was September and we readied ourselves for school. We were to attend the local national school, Scoil Náisiúnta na Rinne. At the convent school we'd attended in Waterford we'd worn slippers and uniforms, comprising brown, pleated gymslips with a sash, and white-buttoned yellow shirts. We'd been instructed in how to sit and stand properly at our desks without making a racket. We never raced in the corridors, even though the floors were perfect sliding places.

The school in the Ring Gaeltacht was a different place entirely for us in the early 1970s. There were boys to begin with, who were foreign beings to me. But it was the girls who won my immediate admiration. There was a blonde-haired girl who stood out for me especially. When the *máistir* (master) stepped out for a few minutes one day, he left her in charge. She was unassailable, standing like a general at the top of the class. She knew how to control all the bold boys. She stood and shouted down the class in clear, authoritative Irish, stilling the hullaballoo with the brilliance and ferocity of her lungs.

'Suigh síos tusa, a amadáin,' she roared at one cheeky imp when he slipped out of his chair. *Sit down, you fool.* Withering him instantly with her contemptuous reprimand, he slumped back into his chair, quietened and defeated.

At lunchtime, there were occasional nettle chases in the yard, when boys went like speed-ships under full throttle, weaving their way in and out through us, waving and brandishing bunches of nettles, trying to whip the legs of unlikely suspects. It was a wild environment for us three shrinking violets, but we loved it. There was the odd rat that scuttled like an old woman across the yard at lunchtime and caused havoc amongst us groups of gossiping young ones. The terror of those mucky, weed-choked corners outside, mixed with the terrible pongs that wafted over us from the *leithreas* (toilet) kept our hearts racing and our eyes alert.

There were exuberant art classes with *an máistir*, Seán de Paor, who was an artist himself and loved to see us painting, and singing classes with the much loved Úna Bean Breathnach, where we played and sang with our hearts thrilling to be reaching such heights of passion. My pulse raced as it had never done before. I ran down like a butterfly across the fields, with my new friend Siobhán gripping my hand to swing me out around her. I bit her finger, biting down on the bone when she tried to smear my face with paint one Friday afternoon, wrapping her fingers around my head from the back. I was ready to kick a boy with venom and ferocity if he fell over on top of his fist of nettles. The place pulsated with energy and vitality and I threw off the yoke of demureness that the nuns had put on me.

Of course, the magic was that everything was through Irish, and in no time I had picked up the most heartfelt terms of abuse and endearment for every occasion: 'Imigh leat, a shíofra' – *go away, you fairy woman*; 'Dún suas, a phleidhce' – *shut up, you messer;* or 'A chailín, a stóirín, a ghrá, cad tá ort?' – *girl, pet, love, what's wrong?* The words wrapped themselves around our days, warming the air like bellows blowing through the slippery boreens.

After a while Ring became home to us. And the longer we stayed, the more familiar everything felt. It's the same today. On Helvick Pier, the forklift whizzes by and cars brake to a halt on the quay. It can sometimes seem busier, but it's the same really. It's the very same as the day we stopped at Robert's Cross to get a look at our new world.

19

Mouse

We hadn't been living long in the country when, one night, just as we settled down to sleep, we heard something scratching away in the corner of our room. Of course we all jumped up on the nearest bed and clung to each other with fright. I stretched across to turn on the light and we scanned the room nervously, straining our ears to make sure we hadn't imagined the noise. No, there it was again. There was a definite scratching going on in the corner. It was exciting and terrifying at the same time.

We zeroed in on the cardboard box we had in the corner as our waste-paper basket. The noise was definitely coming from there. And then we saw it, a tiny little grey creature up on its back legs balancing on top of the cardboard and papers that were in the box, with its pointed face nibbling at something it held steady with its two front legs. The three of us clung to each other and shouted for help as we froze on the bed in terror. Like the great classical statues of Rome, we stood tableau-like, crouched together as one aboard the old-fashioned, spring-based bed. There was the danger we'd topple off the bed and this added to our terror as we swayed horribly with each terrified reaction.

We were in the grip of an irrational, visceral fear to have a mouse so close to us and in our bedroom of all places. It seemed to take hold of us but we could not look away from the mouse's little face as it peeked up and disappeared again.

We saw the crumpled old wrapper from a bar of Cadbury's chocolate move and rustle; the mouse snuffling and rummaging away to its heart's content. It didn't take a blind bit of notice of us.

At this stage, we were screaming in hysterics, shouting instructions at one another to do something. The noise brought our mother. But not being a great lover of mice herself, she stepped back out of the room and called my father. What was all the fuss about, he wanted to know. The three of us pointed to the box in the corner. 'It's a mouse,' we all said. 'Look.'

The poor little mouse was there all right; clear to be seen and oblivious to the mayhem it was causing in our bedroom.

'Put the tennis racket over the box,' said Miriam, pointing to her racket, which was lying on a chair at the door.

'What are you going to do with him, Daddy?' we wanted to know as my father put the racket over the box and took it away with him. As he took control, we were suddenly gripped with concern for the little animal. We trooped after him like the Swiss Family Robinson. Down the stairs we went in single file and huddled in behind him into the bathroom. He put the box in the bath and we all stood back to watch. We wondered what he or the mouse was going to do next. My mother, hoping to regain her standing with us as a courageous heroine, quickly put her hand into the bath, put the stopper in and turned on the tap. As the water filled, the cardboard box began to soften and float. Soon it was all submerged apart from one last pyramid onto which the little mouse clambered to size up his options. He was like Napoleon stranded on his little island of Elba. He seemed to be pleading with us not to let him drown.

'Daddy, he's going to drown,' we shouted as the water rose.

Mouse

'Daddy, look at him.' We all stood around the bath and looked sorrowfully at the mouse. We could see the mouse's little plump body clearly as it balanced itself on the top point of the box and we shivered in sympathy. We began to cry. It was excruciating to watch. We'd been through so much together that by this stage we felt protective towards the creature.

Suddenly the mouse was in the water, swimming away from his little cardboard island. We were sure it was now in imminent danger of drowning. 'Daddy, don't let him drown,' we begged. 'He's only a little mouse.'

In the end, my father caught the mouse by the tail, carried him out to the front door and took him outside to deposit him in a flower bed at the far end of the garden.

'Is he all right?' we asked him when he came back in. 'Will he live?' we wanted to know.

He assured us the mouse would survive and be happy in the garden. We all breathed a sigh of relief as we were whooshed up to bed. As we settled down, we tried not to think about the mouse's family. Would there be little mice babies watching out for him? Would the mouse make it home? How would we ever know his fate?

20

A Dog Named Jingle

Us three little girls didn't quite understand his nature at the start. We tried to groom his wiry hair and tie ribbons around his neck but he wanted no truck with such nonsense. When he was a pup we tried to put him in the pram beside our dolls, only he escaped, leaping out of our arms. We called him Jingle. He was not a Jingle kind of dog. He was a bit like the boy in the Johnny Cash song 'A Boy Named Sue', who had to be manly and virile enough to carry off the name.

Of the three dogs we ever had, the one my father loved best of all was this black and white mongrel, a squat dog, who was part Jack Russell and had eyes of bog-like opaqueness and a little docked tail that stood upright at the end of his body in a most unattractive manner. Jingle was no oil painting but he was an integral part of our family for almost fifteen years. He had his own spot on the mat each evening in front of the fire.

He was a loyal family pet. He came with us from our home in the city to the very different seaside environment of the Ring peninsula. It was a great odyssey and he took possession of his new terrain with a swagger and a great deal of self-assurance. There were strange smells from pats of steaming cow dung, boxes of rotting fish, crabs to worry and horses of which to be wary. Like any male dog, he was largely focused on food, bitches in heat and his master's call. For him the priorities never wavered – territory, survival and fornication.

A Dog Named Jingle

During the day, he took up sentry duty on the garden wall at the front of the house in Baile na nGall. He vetted all passers-by, viewing any movement or change on the horizon carefully with a shrewd eye, only lifting his head from the wall for some, while for others he'd jump down and go over for a sniff of inspection. Then he'd swagger back, jump back up onto the wall and resume his position.

Due to a blow from a passing car once, he loathed all manner of vehicles – tractors, bread vans, estate cars, lorries, motor cycles – no moving machine was safe. As a locomotive approached, he'd spring into action, priming himself in readiness to give chase. We lived at a crossroads so Jingle never knew what direction the car was going to take when it reached our junction and so he'd begin turning early, wheeling again and again in readiness for his take-off up one of the roads or downhill towards the pier in hot pursuit of the vehicle. To the uninitiated, it looked as if he was just spinning like a top, chasing his tail to bite it. As the car braked or accelerated, he'd whirl in ever-tighter circles, with an ever-increasing degree of urgency and excitement, looking more and more like a whirling dervish spinning on a pin. Once the car had taken the bend, he'd accelerate up the road after them, warning them off our patch, barking and harrying the wheels of the car, engaged in a lecture of outrage.

Although he particularly loathed cars, he also guarded against intruders who happened to walk onto our forecourt. My father had a small grocery shop so we had plenty of customers passing in and out, and mostly Jingle showed great forbearance, but there was the occasional customer who just seemed to rub him up the wrong way. Call it a clash of personalities, but there were those who loved to engage him in an angry exchange. Then we'd see him bare his crooked, gapped teeth and adopt his most ferocious pose with the hairs up on the back of his neck to emit a growl that grew in intensity.

'Aaaaagh, go way out a' that,' the passing neighbour might say as he went down the road.

A car got him in the end, though, and my father had to carry him in and bury him in the garden out the back. Afterwards, he stood at the sink for a while looking out the window across the bay towards the Comeraghs. Us girls didn't stop our chatter until we saw his shoulders twitching and we noticed something was not quite right.

'The poor hoor,' my father cried, his hands lifting up to his eyes.

It was only then I realised how he'd lost a friend, how they'd been together all through the years, two males, allies united, in a house full of women.

21

Joe

We usually met on important family occasions in our aunts' sitting room in Helvick, which was about two miles further along the road from us at the furthest point on the peninsula. As a treat, us girls would always have Barley's lime cordial, while my mother would have some cherry brandy and my father and uncle had Guinness and some whiskey. My aunts only drank tea.

We loved our visits to Helvick because we could listen to the adults talking about old times and, of course, we took part in the sing-song when it started.

My Uncle Joe was usually called on to sing first because he loved to and because his voice was rich and melodious. He relished singing and he had a store of songs that he'd learned from listening to artists like Johnny Cash and Jim Reeves. Roger Whittaker's 'The Last Farewell' was one of his favourites. After a swallow of Guinness to soothe his throat, he'd put his glass down carefully on the coffee table and compose himself. His face would take on a dreamy, serious expression. Then he'd lift his head and begin – his deep, rich voice filling the room with the music and the story:

> *There's a ship lies rigged and ready in the harbour,*
> *Tomorrow for old England she sails.*

We loved this song because it told a story. I especially enjoyed the chorus with its lilting, easy melody.

For you are beaut–i–ful,
And I have loved you dearly,
More dearly than the spoken word can tell.

We were hooked from the start of 'The Last Farewell'. A ring of stout around his mouth was a sign that Joe was truly in the moment and it seemed to add to the piquancy of the words because there was a sadness about Joe that none of us young people could ever miss. And that none of us ever came close to understanding.

We all joined in at the chorus, singing along with Joe. The fact that Uncle Joe was a merchant seaman and fisherman who had gone to sea as a young man, working on ocean liners and oil rigs and trawlers, seemed to give the song an added pathos. He had never married and I always felt that when he sang those songs of lost love, it was heartfelt in some way.

There was a vulnerability and an incongruity about Joe that made me feel slightly embarrassed sometimes. The angelic quality of his voice and his open trusting eyes seemed to ask a question that sometimes left me feeling sad. As he sang, he'd lift his head up at certain parts, almost in sympathy with the fate of the tragic sailor, to check to see if we understood. Time slowed down as his voice filled the room.

Joe had thick black eyebrows over dark-brown eyes that seemed to hold your gaze when he looked at you in moments of honest appraisal. He had a head of rich dark-brown hair, a strong jawline and a fine profile. He was handsome in a rough, masculine way. He smoked Major cigarettes and the tops of the fingers on his left hand were brown from years of holding the stubs in his hand.

Joe

He walked with a limp, and one shoe was always built up by the cobbler to compensate for the shorter leg that had shrivelled when he was in his late teens. It was many years before we learned that this wastage of the bone could sometimes happen, in particular to young men, following intense physical activity. We knew Joe had cycled a lot and played a great deal of hurling as a young man, so we presumed that this was how it had happened. Because of this wastage, Joe sat in the armchair in his own characteristic way, with one leg outstretched and the shorter leg folded under him.

Those times remain clear in my memory now: of Joe singing with emotion of other worlds and times. Looking out the window in Helvick, I remember the grey-green sea stretching off down the coastline to the east, towards Hook Head in the distance and the town of Dungarvan visible in the west. I can see the seagulls following in the wake of an occasional trawler.

Joe seemed to favour songs about loneliness, about drinking and about disappointment. He loved songs by the American singer Jim Reeves. 'I asked the man,' he'd sing, 'behind the bar, for the juke-box, and the music takes me back to Tennessee.' He used to lift his shoulders in a semi-shrug as he sang the last line: 'When they ask, who's the fool in the cor-ner cry-ing, I say, little ole wine drinker me.'

Now the words and the music of the songs he sang merge like a collage of melodies into one: the notes unfolding slowly in my head, Joe's voice rising effortlessly. Unhurried, he'd pause like any singer if a long breath were required. He'd often close his eyes but sometimes he'd look into the near distance as he put his heart into the words.

Years later, he lay in hospital smiling like a baby, his eyes clear like an infant staring out from a pram. His memory was gone and his words were all fragmented or lost, but the nurses were always kind to him and often asked to see photographs of him as a young man because they could see how handsome he must have been and they responded to an innocence in his eyes.

He died in his late sixties in hospital. We buried him on an icy cold day in January. There were hailstones and yet the freezing air that day on the exposed coastal graveyard seemed right somehow.

Like the words of the song of 'The Last Farewell', which Roger Whittaker sang in the 1970s, I felt he had gone away to a land full of endless sunshine and left the 'rainy skies and gales'. On that last day in the cemetery, when I said goodbye to Uncle Joe, I remembered him singing 'The Last Farewell' in Helvick and all of a sudden the words came back to me as if he was there beside me, smiling.

22

Sheila

I only heard my Auntie Sheila sing once and I remember the occasion clearly. It was wintertime. We had gathered together for her birthday. We'd been their neighbours in Ring for a few years at this point and a tradition to visit them on such occasions had already been established.

We had cake and drinks and we gave her presents. The cold outside was kept at bay by heavy curtains and a fire burned away in the grate. All the wrapping paper from the presents was folded and put in a pile at her feet. Bubble bath, slippers and a new hot water bottle were ranged around her – valued gifts from her three nieces.

We performed our party pieces from a selection that included 'The Mountains of Mourne' and 'Drumcolliher' by Percy French, as well as more up-to-date ones by the Clancys and others. We sang Irish songs too – 'Buachaill ón Éirne' and 'A Chomaraigh Aoibhinn O' – and my father with his halting rendition of 'Dear Old Home' brought a lump to my throat. We all joined in for the chorus: 'Dear old home, far across the sea, day and night to thee I'm sadly yearning,' and the words were so familiar to us: 'how I long to see the dear old home again, the cottage down the little winding glen, I can see the roses climbing, I can hear the church bell chiming and I long to see the dear old home again.'

The party was at a point when the energy was in danger

of ebbing away unless somebody stepped in to provide an additional turn. In desperation our eyes turned to Auntie Sheila. Perhaps she'd play the violin, which she did on rare occasions. At first she was adamant that she would not. But then, after some persuasion, she seemed to relent somewhat and said she'd sing 'Whispering Hope', as she had come across the words in a newspaper cutting for just such an occasion.

She put her cup of tea down, patted her hair, rummaged in her handbag and pulled out a wallet. After going through all the little pockets, she found the words and she stood to perform.

There was a warm glow in the sitting room in Helvick as Sheila stood. Sheila's sister, Gile, sat at the opposite side of the fireplace, sipping tea. The two of them loved to host any kind of a party and we loved going as they dressed up for the occasion – as did we – and we were given preferential treatment.

Sheila stood near the lamp so that she could read the small print. She took a breath. The first tentative notes to emerge were flute-like in quality. I recall being afraid that stage fright would take hold of her.

'Soft as the voice of an angel, breathing a lesson unheard,' she sang. The sound of her voice was like a whisper, yet it somehow came out clear and sure. We didn't make a sound as we listened.

After years of smoking Silk Cut cigarettes, her voice was reedy and thin. As she reached for the high notes, her hand went up to her throat. She ran out of breath once or twice but still the notes came, shrill and pipe-like, as if blown in by the wind.

I can still see Auntie Sheila, pale-skinned with blue-rinsed hair styled in soft waves over her head, standing there under the lamp. After being widowed at a young age, she had retired to Helvick. She never remarried.

Sheila

'Wait till the darkness is over, wait till the tempest is done,' she sang. The magic stole over me and wove its spell. I continue to love this hymn.

As we drove home to Baile na nGall that night, the words of 'Whispering Hope' stayed with us, and the trembling voice of Auntie Sheila singing about hope, cautioning us to wait till the tempest is over, became part of the night. The unfairness of her own fate, widowed at a young age, seemed to suit the song. The soothing quality in her voice, 'soft like the voice of an angel', seemed to echo through the darkness as we drove further and further away from Helvick.

When the dark midnight is over
Watch for the breaking of day.
Whispering hope, o how gentle thy voice,
Making my heart in its sorrow rejoice.

23

Harold

Harold Kenneth Long, a native of Youghal, was married to my lovely Aunt Sheila. He was a much-loved only child, who grew up in a privileged Protestant home in Longville House in Co. Cork. He is buried in the grounds of St Mary's Church in Youghal.

I never knew him but over the years I've seen many photographs of him and of his parents. I often wonder what Harold was like in person. We have a photograph of him as a young man. He's sitting on a Lilo – a type of inflated rubber mattress – on a beach. He looks relaxed and happy. He's slim and pleasant looking. He may even have been handsome. He's neatly dressed in a soft-buttoned shirt and creased trousers. He looks kind.

Do I read too much into the remnants of his life that have come into my possession? Harold's father wrote to Sheila in December 1942, introducing himself and 'suggesting to adopt you as our only daughter and offer you all a daughter should have in our home'.

Harold died before he and Sheila could have any children. He was only a young man in his thirties at the time of his death. They had been married only a few short years when he died tragically.

He must have played the piano as I have some sheet music of his, dating from the 1920s. The sheets are dusty and faded but still so redolent of the gay twenties, that time between the wars when the Charleston and the two-step were in vogue. There's

Harold

'Panama Twilight', words by Wilder D'Lea, music by Fisher Thompson, where 'the orchids, dear, are blooming once again … In Old Panama I long to dwell. I want to see your smiles of love divine, kiss your lips and hear you say "you're mine", beneath the starry sky.'

I imagine Harold as being very debonair and rather dashing, with a cravat, crisply pressed trousers and squeaking new leather shoes. He was a banker. I know he was a gardener, too, because he died from tetanus poisoning after pruning roses in their garden in Blackrock. His untimely demise might easily have been written into a Noël Coward play, such was its tragic and yet theatrically rapid onset.

I wonder if he serenaded my Aunt Sheila during their courtship. Sheila played the piano and the violin. Did they ever play duets together, I wonder? It was a rare occurrence for Sheila to play in later life. It seemed to cause her distress even to think about taking the fiddle out of its case.

There's a drawing of a couple on the cover of another piece of sheet music that Harold owned. I gaze at their old-fashioned pose – the couple is gauche and fey, airy and fantastical. The song is about a girl called Mabel, entitled 'Why Did I Kiss that Girl'. It's a whimsical piece, with words by Lew Brown and music by Robert King and Ray Henderson. From the 1920s, it's signed by Harold and dated 8 August 1924. Did he play this song in Longville as the summer sun threw dappled light across the terrace when the evening was coming in slowly over the bay? According to the song:

> Bashful Johnny Green just turned seventeen …
> Some dear friends he knew introduced him to Mabel at a dance

She was very nice so he kissed her twice ...
In the morning, all his friends heard Bashful Johnny say,

'O, why did I kiss that girl? Why oh why, oh why
Why did I kiss that girl? I could almost cry
I'm nervous, so nervous, I'm worried and blue
And if her kiss did that what would her huggin' do?'

And so it continued, each line funnier than the last.

I've inherited some of his books too, such as *Dear Ducks*, which is one of thirteen volumes about the fictional locale of Ballygullion in the Slievegullion region of County Down. Lynn Doyle, a banker in Dublin, wrote it. I think he and Harold must have been friends as they shared similar Anglo-Irish backgrounds and careers. The book is signed by Harold and dated 24 January 1934. His signature is tight and discrete. It's careful and precise with small and neat letters.

I wish I had known him, this man who loved books and played music. I'd like to ask him if he watched over Sheila all her life while she bided her time, waiting to join him. Perhaps I'm being fanciful.

I turn the pages of Sheila's old photograph albums, wanting to unearth another particle of information about Harold and his life. And I turn the pages of his books in the hope of catching a glimpse of his long ago youth.

I wonder if he had a good voice. I spot a mark in the margin, or a dog-eared page and I wait for it to reveal something new to me. These remnants of another life leave me puzzling over them for a long time, until sometimes I catch a slipstream of intuition and ride it, letting my imagination run riot.

24

Boarding School

It was my aunts who took me to Cork to have me fitted out in a brown gymslip for boarding school in Ardfoyle on the banks of the Lee. They paid for the blazer with the school crest on it too. They judged the effect, turning me around to study the cut of the uniform on my little twelve-year-old frame. They tightened the sash and fixed the pleats and I felt like an experiment as they lavished me with the best of everything, even treating me to tea in the Walter Raleigh Hotel in Youghal on our way home.

I arrived home laden down with a great pile of parcels and bags. Of course my younger sisters were green with envy as I paraded around in my new uniform and gabardine coat. All belted up in the brown ensemble, I tightened the buckle, placed the school beret at a jaunty angle atop my head and swaggered around like Marlene Dietrich playing Mata Hari.

As I counted the days until I'd be driven to my new school some sixty miles away, I sewed special name tags onto everything – a new pair of sheets, two new linen napkins, two new blankets, a Foxford rug and a little grey games skirt with a swish that I could easily see myself wearing when I went out with my first ever hockey stick onto the playing pitch. I'd be saying goodbye to the rough and tumble of camogie matches in the Gaeltacht. It would be a life of hockey games, sports mistresses and midnight feasts, just like in Enid Blyton's *Malory Towers* or *St Clare's*. I started thinking about tuck boxes and I wondered if they'd have a sports' hall, a belfry or a matron for when I was sent to the infirmary.

My initials were carved into my own cutlery set and I got a heavy silver table-ring for my two new linen napkins. And Auntie Sheila gave me a great American suitcase with fading labels pasted on its sides, mementoes of her exotic honeymoon cruise to New York and other trips to Corfu and Rome. As I packed the case – with four new vests, eight pants, half a dozen brown knee-socks, the school tie, my new dressing gown, slippers and a toilet bag – I felt my own journey to faraway Cork and the boarding school was well on a par with such travels. My life would be spectacular, worth writing about in a novel, like the life of Jane Eyre, The Little Madeleine or Anne of Green Gables.

And in the end it was as good as any Enid Blyton novel – we had Miss Fiona Walton for English, Mr O'Driscoll for history, tobogganing during the snow and a head girl to lead us in grace before meals. I woke every morning to the sound of bells being rung up and down the dormitory aisles. After breakfast, we'd shiver on the avenue walk to our classrooms, the crunch of gravel cracking like ice underfoot in the eerie stillness of the morning. At night we'd gather in the refectory, deafening ourselves as we dragged our 200 stools from under the tables to sit as one for dinner.

Still, nothing could compare with being home for Christmas. I sat at the kitchen table, watching my mother shake the flour loose and kneading the dough as she made brown bread – a knot in my stomach as I felt the days slip away. I tiptoed around in case it was a dream. My sisters in turn tiptoed around me. In a way I was like a stranger in their midst.

Boarding School

All too quickly the Christmas holidays were over and I was back at school again, suspended in that strange school universe, adrift at night in a sea of echoing silence.

By the start of the second term I knew all too well the daily rituals of boarding school, as well as the longing, loneliness and wishing that went with it. At bedtime in my little cubicle, even as I tried to damp down the waves of homesickness, a terrible tide of longing would sweep me along. The only relief for homesickness came on Sunday afternoons at exactly 3 p.m. when I would stand on the convent landing and focus all my attention on the public payphone.

Its sudden explosion into life was terrifying but I'd pick up the receiver and hear my mother's voice. Then a tightness would grip my chest and I'd lose the ability to speak, at first, but as tears streamed out of my eyes, I would give vent to the great river of loss that my twelve-year-old self could hardly understand.

25

Boys

I began to notice boys at a young age. I'm not sure if it was out of innocent curiosity or because of the early onset of carnal desire. Anyway, two little boys from Liverpool, home on holidays in August, used to play near us on the breakwater in Passage East where we used to spend all our holidays when we lived in Waterford. Was it their blond hair, their strange accents, their athleticism or their smart clothes that caught my attention first? All I remember is that the sun shone when they appeared. I used to see their little legs and elbows going like pistons as I watched from a discreet distance.

When I was about nine I remember being shy, being interested and wondering how I could get closer to these intriguing specimens of Liverpudlian boyhood. I recall watching them covertly from the storm wall that ran along by the cockle walk. Of course, this was an unspoken passion and, sadly, my presence remained unmarked by them. During this time I was also charged with keeping an eye on my two younger sisters and while I issued instructions to them about holding my hand when crossing to the shop, or asked them for another candy cigarette or jelly baby, I was all the while aware of the two golden-haired, brown-kneed gods who sat on high atop the breakwater, watching the tide turn and the waves break on the strand. My pulse seemed to quicken at the sight of them and my awareness of their proximity was acute.

Then there was Jacko the Monkey. Of course my two siblings, to my great annoyance, had great fun teasing me about him. They would call to tell me he had just passed our house in Waterford, that he had looked in or that he had stopped to ask my mother a question. Jacko the Monkey, they would sing. I used to blush on having my barely expressed, barely formed interest so rudely unmasked. And my interest in this young man, who used to sell badges for the scouts, was so fleeting that he's hardly worth a mention; it was only that a mention of his nickname or a sighting of his distant figure cycling up John's Hill was enough to have my sisters in giggles.

It was when I was at boarding school in Cork that I discovered Donny Osmond, a key figure in my development as a teenager. He was all the rage in the early 1970s. While I was there I had a photograph of this pouting, dark-haired singer surrounded by his large family in pride of place on my bedside table. I had the black and white photo in a little stand-alone picture frame.

I recall the head nun coming to visit me in my cubicle once when I was sick in bed. She saw the picture and smiled indulgently.

'Is that the family?' she asked me gently.

'Yes, Sister,' I told her, glancing briefly at Donny and the rest of the Osmonds, not wanting to draw too much attention to this figure of desire. 'And where are you?' she asked me and so, to my embarrassment, I had to explain who he was.

After I had spent two years at the boarding school in Cork, it closed – much to the disappointment of my younger sisters who thought they'd never get to experience for themselves the 'joys' of midnight feasts, tuck boxes and long weekends away from home. I came home to attend the all-girl Presentation Convent Secondary School. This involved more girls, more nuns and, consequently, there was a period when I worried that there was surely a dearth of similarly aged young men in the world, as I was not meeting any of them. I came to believe that none existed and I told myself that I should accept my fate.

And thus it wasn't until I grew up and learned to break the sound barrier that I spoke to these gods of allure, of maleness, of beauty. To me, boys are figures of romance and adventure. Boys in my eyes will always be mysterious, unknowable and distant. Thank heavens for their *seeming* indifference, perched high on a breakwater and gazing out to sea. Thank heavens for their difference, for their ability to remain aloof and fleeting, and for all their strange, otherworldly qualities.

26

Summer Songs

The songs of the McGarrigles wafted out from the Yellow House all during the hot days in Ring in the summer of 1976. These Canadian sisters were singer-songwriters, who often sang about swimming – 'when I did the backstroke and the butterfly and the old Australian crawl'; they sang about leaving and bidding farewell; they sang about the blues – 'never having had the blues from whence I came but in New York state, I caught 'em' – and their pure voices wrapped themselves around my heart 'like a wheel out in mid ocean'.

Our cousin Donal Musgrave and his family came on holiday to Ring that year. He, his wife Shirley and their two children, Katie and Darragh, rented the Yellow House, which stood overlooking the cove and was perched at the very edge of the cliff. Even as we lolled on the grass on the slope underneath the Yellow House and looked down onto the stony inlet of the cove which nestles under Helvick Head, we could hear the Mc-Garrigles singing. And from the start I loved their songs.

The house was a former hunting lodge belonging to the Villiers Stuart family, which dated back to the eighteenth century. It was said to be haunted but the Musgraves weren't afraid of any ghosts. No matter how many warning, big-eyed glances we'd give them, they settled in happily, braving those rooms we found cold and creepy. They never seemed to notice the chill you'd feel when you stood for a moment in a corner.

They were planning to stay for a month. On arrival, they draped their togs along the banisters of the minstrel's gallery and put all their Wellingtons and fishing rods, their buckets and spades along the wall near the wainscoting. They were our sophisticated city cousins, and all through that summer of 1976 when I heard the McGarrigles playing on their stereo, my breath caught in my throat and I stood rooted to the spot, looking out over the deep green depths of the little stony strand beneath, listening to the plaintive notes of 'Go, leave, don't come back, no more am I for the taking, but I can't say that my heart's not aching, it's breaking in two'.

I had come of age listening to the *sean-nós* and all the great songs of loneliness, loss and deportation, such as 'Na Conneries', 'Sliabh Geal gCua' and 'A Chumaraigh Aoibheann Ó'. But that summer the McGarrigles blew like a fresh summer breeze across my bow and I was buoyed up and rocked away over the waves to a bright, sunlit place where I could be sixteen and trembling, fresh and new. They helped me find my own voice. Their harmonies wedded themselves to my ear, the pitch and timbre of their voices matched my own exactly. I bought my own tape and wore it out listening to them.

My mother loved the light, airy swing of 'Foolish You' – 'Sad and foolish that's how I feel, don't you know how fortune favours few, fortune's blind, as blind as you my dear, what a pity, oh foolish you'. Sing that for me, she'd say and away I'd go, like Kate and Anna McGarrigle, singing with my heart until my voice caught as I reached a top note.

I filled our kitchen with the cool summer sounds of their songs until they became part of our repertoire, sisters like us, who were 'like interlocking pieces in the jigsaw puzzle of life', as one of their songs described.

'Talk to me of Mendocino' was so strange and ethereal sounding. Where was Mendocino? I hardly know still, but it cast a spell, like 'My Town', which told of someone who 'had to leave it and head south where the climate is kind'. Or 'Go Leave' and its description of a heart that was 'breaking in two'. It was the instruments they played that beguiled as much as their voices – there was a banjo, symbols, a tambourine, a harmonium, a mandolin and a melodeon. As they drew out those long notes like a piece of string, those old-fashioned instruments resonated and harkened back to years before when my father had played the melodeon, or the tremolo of my mother's plucking when she picked out the notes of 'The Croppy Boy' on her mandolin.

I loved their harmonies, their swerving changes of key and their notes that dipped and rose like rearing horses. The McGarrigles sounded like they came from a family who sang old-fashioned hymns and parlour songs and gathered around an organ in the wilds of Quebec.

Such pathos and such words in both English and French held me in thrall. Their singing sounded unbounded and raw, and implicit in their songs and the way they sang them was the story of their own flight from home to find their feet.

27

Swan Song

There was a hum of conversation in Murray's when we went in on that particular morning, a buzz of excitement, *mar bhí cuairteoirí tagtha* – as visitors had arrived. These visitors had attracted musicians from the area to gather in the pub. Expectation of the great entertainment that was to come was in the air. Raconteurs were vying with each other to take centre stage; tin whistles, bodhráns and fiddles were ready to burst forth and laughter rose in bubbles with local fishermen mixing with the visiting revellers.

It was my father's habit to go to the pub for a drink on a Sunday morning before dinner. I was with him on this occasion. He chatted to some friends at the counter so I left him and sat staring out the window at the overcast day. The sea was a rumpled sheet of pale jade moving silently across the bay.

As it happens, I found myself sitting next to the great musician and piper Séamus Ennis. He had a slow, graceful manner. I was also aware of his towering reputation as a collector of folklore. I knew that he was a lover of *sean-nós* and that he was a gifted performer himself. He was greatly admired in our Gaeltacht area, but I was a teenager at the time so I stayed quiet on the edge of the company.

He was gracious when he sat down beside me to say hello. He was in a black suit and he wore spectacles. He had a high forehead and hollow cheeks. His unbelievably long, pale fingers rested on the stops of the uilleann pipes, which were strapped to his shoulder and arm.

I was struck by the kindness and attractiveness in his face.

He spoke with a low, gravelly voice. His eyes were full of wonder and barely concealed merriment. He was compelling and he spoke in clear, tuneful Irish. As a collector of *béaloideas*, i.e. folklore, who had cycled and driven to cottages all over the country from the 1940s onwards, he was an old hand at putting people of all ages at their ease.

Had I ever heard of the story of the dying swan, he asked me. The swan is known to sing only once in its life, he said. She sings when she is about to die, he explained. He watched my reaction.

It seemed as if no one else in the pub was listening when he spoke to me. The tragedy and beauty of the fable gripped me instantly. 'The swan sings "Cuimhe cí, cuimhe có",' he said. 'Have you heard it?' I shook my head. He sang it softly then. 'Cuimhe cí, cuimhe có, cuimhe có. That's the sound a swan makes at the end,' he explained.

His voice, a deep bass tremolo was musical, low and evocative. He sang those notes of requiem slowly and, like a whisper, they went into my ear and stirred my imagination. It was a lament by a swan whose nest has been plundered. In my mind's eye I could see the ageing swan somewhere on a darkening lake, gliding through lonely reeds and then coming to the bank to climb ashore cumbersomely, her head stooped low as she prepared to die.

Ennis and myself sat side by side on a bench in Murray's, the sea behind us, the mountains in the distance reaching up through the clouds: the view, timeless and serene, in keeping with the swan's last notes. And with the fierce intensity of feeling that all teenagers experience, I was both fascinated and horrified by this beautifully sad image of death.

Then, giving resonance and depth to his voice, he played the dying notes of the air on the pipes, and their low breathy drone added to the terrible grief of the dying swan as she laid her head down to leave the world in all its beauty.

I came across a recording of Séamus Ennis recently on YouTube where he is playing a reel that was composed by his father, James Ennis, around 1913. It's called 'The Morning Thrush'. He says a thrush that sang on a tree outside the window inspired his father, and that he himself then heard a thrush at home and he could hear some of the phrases his father had composed in the bird's singing. I continue to search but have so far failed to find a recording of him playing or singing 'Cuimhe cí, cuimhe có'.

The diaries Séamus Ennis kept when he worked for the Irish Folklore Commission between 1942 and 1946 are published in a book called *Mise an Fear Ceoil* by Cló Iar-Chonnacht. The author, Ríonach Uí Ogáin, includes plenty of insights and stories. 'Tá scéilíní ann faoina chlisteacht, faoina cheol agus faoina dhathúlacht' – *there are stories there about his intelligence, about his music and about his attractiveness*, she writes.

Although I've never heard 'Cuimhe cí, cuimhe có' since, the few moments I spent with him that day have stayed in my memory, clear as a bell – like a perfect note.

28

My Aunts

My two aunts, Sheila and Gile, often sat at our fireplace, sipping tea delicately from china cups. They would take long draws from their cigarettes and regale us with anecdotes and conversation. One story sparked off another.

They told us stories of long ago, of family escapades in Ferrybank where they grew up, of old beaux and dances, of summer nights at the traditional céilí dances in Ring where they spent their holidays, and other stories that had stayed with them over the years. They used to tell us stories both about and against themselves, about trips they'd made to Rome or people they'd met in Lourdes.

Once in a while one of them would excuse herself to 'spend a penny', as they euphemistically described a trip to the bathroom. In the meantime, the other aunt would carry on with the anecdotes, not missing a beat.

We loved to sit around the fire, listening to them, entranced by their conversation and their turn of phrase. And they loved to hold court. The room would fill with smoke, the taste of tannin hung in the air and the walls were warm to the touch. Once Sheila had finished, Gile would take up the thread and their talk of days gone by would continue. When they got up to go, we'd all heave ourselves up, wishing they didn't have to go, and we'd accompany them outside to their car, a sporty little coupé.

My aunts were authorities on everything. I usually sat on the hearth as close to the heat as possible, like a cat purring, with my knees under my chin, listening to them. My two sisters usually sat as close to them as possible also, on the mat or on the arm of a chair. We drew in close to listen and egg them on, ready to provide the required 'What happened then?' when the moment demanded it. They could just as easily comment on what we wore, or ask how we were doing at school. But such was our addiction to their company that we were prepared to take that risk and put up with such inquisitions.

Perhaps it was their certainty about everything that we liked. There were no half measures or shades of grey. They had rules and there were no prevarications or hesitations. As long as they stayed by the fire drinking tea, talking to us, lecturing us even, we'd listen, waiting to jump in order to replenish their tea and keep their stories going. Their arrival heralded a break from the daily routine.

It was like that the day I made the fatal mistake of letting it slip that I was not going across to the nightly céilí in the local hall. They were not at all pleased with this but I was in my mid-teens at the time and not inclined to attend these dances of public embarrassment and bewilderment.

'Would you like another hot drop?' I asked them, hoping to distract them from my non-appearances at the céilí. Sheila held out her cup, like a queen who was happy to indulge me. She waited while I poured. It acted as a pause in the dramatic yarn she was in the midst of telling. We all waited quietly, hanging on her every word and exhalation of smoke.

Despite my best efforts, they turned their attention away from their story. The two of them eyed one another across the mat. Sheila's eyes grew round and her eyebrows raised a fraction. Gile sucked in her lips in disapproval.

'He won't come down the chimney to you, you know!' Aunty Sheila declared, her face scowling at the terrible fate that was in store for me should such a calamity as not going to the céilí become a regular occurrence. While she began to recount a story of moonlit nights on the way home from the céilí with boys they knew, I looked dolefully at the chimney in front of me and sheepishly agreed to go to the céilí from then on.

Their visits are vignettes in my mind. I've clear memories of the two of them, sitting in the prime seats at either side of the fireside, regaling us with their wit and their wisdom, the room full of their presence.

Today, we still sit around the fire, talking about the garden, about work, about shopping and whatever news is doing the rounds. We huddle around the fire and enjoy the shelter the house provides from the icy breeze outside. We are filled with a sense that this room has been at the centre of our lives for decades. We've spent evenings and nights putting more coal on the fire, plumping up the cushions and making ourselves comfortable, and often, when we think back, our circle resonates again with those conversations and oft-told stories and the fireside is peopled with vivid memories of my two aunts with their cups of tea and their cigarettes daintily held aloft.

29

The Boys from Bagenalstown

After my return from boarding school, my parents decided they'd prefer to have my sisters and I at home with them; therefore, rather than look for another boarding school, they sent us all to the local Presentation Convent in Dungarvan, which had both a primary and a secondary school on the same site. From then on, at the beginning of the new school year, we were all kitted out in new navy uniforms and driven in for the start of school at 9 a.m.

Winters took on a new routine during this time. Flooding on the road, drifts of snow, or cows on their way back to graze, as well as the vagaries of the battery in our old car, all conspired to delay us on different occasions on our journey to school.

After the end of school each day, we'd pile into the car waiting at the school gate and head home, full of the day's adventures. Our evenings were taken up with television, dinner, homework and bed. In school we moved from classrooms to science labs, from the assembly hall to stairwells and cloakrooms. We stood at our desks and said a prayer at the start of each class. We became familiar with the words of Shakespeare's two heroines, Rosaline and Celia, in *As You Like It*. We read stories in Irish by writers such as Pádraig Ó Conaire and Pádraig Mac Piarais; we had isosceles triangles and myriad other mysteries of geometry explained to us. We studied European history and covered milestones such as the Second World War, the Renaissance and the Industrial

Revolution. We read poems by Yeats, Kavanagh and Keats. We learned by rote and sometimes by logic. We had a number of lay teachers but we also had several brilliant religious teachers, including Sr de Lourdes, Sr Mary of the Sacred Heart, Mother Margaret Mary, Sr Maria Gioretti, Sr Perpetua and Sr Gertrude.

One evening I was recruited for the debating team by Sr de Lourdes. I didn't realise at the time that the world was within the grasp of this debating team, that we were about to step out onto the public stage and that soon we'd be winning debating competitions and returning victorious to our school.

In due course, it came to be and word was sent around that all classes were to gather in the assembly hall. We stood apart on the stage and saw the students file in. The noise as they shuffled in grew in intensity until the principal had no choice but to call everyone to order.

'Settle down, girls,' she instructed, her voice like a bell above the racket. 'I have a special announcement'. A hush descended on the school population. All eyes were upon us, smiling and grateful for the change of tempo in the school on a Thursday morning when any distraction from the humdrum daily grind of learning was welcomed by teachers and pupils alike.

Now they looked up at us, the debating team, and after the principal announced news of our win, thunderous applause broke out. We'd come back as the provincial champions after beating the Ursulines, the convent girls from the city. We'd won the Junior Chamber Ireland Regional Debating Final. We were the toast of the school. A photographer from the local paper was waiting in the wings. We were front-page news that week in *The Dungarvan Leader*. *The Dungarvan Observer* and *The Munster Express* had the story as well.

'Would you look at the cut of her hair,' one girl said in a whisper within hearing of my youngest sister. Ignoring the disparaging reference to my untidy appearance, she quipped proudly, 'That's my sister.'

Our next bout of debating would be against the boys of St Joseph's Academy in Bagenalstown at the All-Ireland quarter-final. Strangely, we didn't rate them at all. We viewed them as country boys, not equal to us sophisticates, girls from the Presentation Convent in West Waterford. We felt unbeatable in our navy skirts and blazers emblazoned with the school crest and our ties of silver and blue.

In the heat of debate we were all eager protestations and declamatory statements. At full tilt, we'd hold our prompt cards out like tear-stained hankies and we'd plead our case: 'Madam chairman, reverend sisters, friends, ladies and gentlemen, members of the opposition, I tell you the place of justice is a hallowed place.'

We'd raise our arms in oratorical excess and hammer home our points. We knew how to frown dramatically – all scrunched-up eyebrows and lined foreheads – in order to achieve maximum expressions of shock and concern. We had the debating lingo down pat. We were praised in the local press for the 'power of our logical aggression and teamwork'.

Such was our ease that on the night of beating the much-feared girls' debating team from Killarney in the Munster semi-final, one of my teammates, Sheila, mid-opening address, hardly missed a beat even when a little mouse ran across the stage. We, her fellow teammates, were equally still; such was the level of our commitment and concentration.

'Madam chairman, reverend sisters, friends, ladies and

gentlemen, members of the proposing team, I strongly oppose the motion that pollution is the price of progress.'

Night after night, we'd stay back after school with Sr de Lourdes to hone our arguments and ready ourselves to do battle with the upcoming opposition. On the night of a debate, we'd bombard the audience with our brilliance.

We had a strong sense that our fellow students and our teachers supported us. We were showered with compliments and idolatrous glances whenever we walked through the school. Teaching nuns stopped us to ask us questions about our progress.

Our prowess on the debating floor was a whispered legend. We were the special ones, an elite bunch, famed for our intellects, our rapier wit and logic.

The boys of Bagenalstown, we were sure, would be a piece of cake. We were half-embarrassed on their behalf at the cruel treatment they would receive at our hands, such was our self-belief.

And so we travelled to Bagenalstown. They were dishevelled when they walked out, shy and stumbling even. We noted the curled-up edges of their off-white collars, and the way their ties hung loosely around their necks.

We took our places and the debate began.

We were smug at the start, but we quickly realised how stunningly brilliant they were as our polished gestures and words were batted away like stray balls on a tennis court. Their arguments pulverised us. They were mercurial and gauche, sharp and incisive. And as our arguments drew to an end, we were left winded, well and truly knocked off our perch by the boys from Bagenalstown, who ran away with the motion and ended our run of debating successes.

Beyond the Breakwater

As we drove home in the minibus that night, we feared we would never know those heights of idolatry or fame again.

Sisters

Cream cheeks; thin, delicate thighs;
pinched-at-you-looking eyes;
Whinging and writhing now and then,
with a hot water bottle under the quilt.
Then 'Kitty, rub my back'.
This is the silkiest time.
Sitting on the pillow, my palm rubbing her back,
pressing her better.
Waiting.
I rub fast, hard, as she tenses
from the pain
and the wincing shoots through to her shins.
It eases.
And quietens
as both of us: you lying, I sitting,
breathing, in thought, in time,
wait at home under the skylight,
still as the clouds that pass by.

The Pope's Visit

We left while it was still dark and wintry, piling into a minibus up on the Helvick Road. We were still half asleep – us three sisters with fellow teenagers of the parish all under the care of our local curate. Each of us had sandwiches and crisps and flasks of tea. My mother had made a banner using an old sheet and sewn a wide strip of yellow felt material as a border around its edge so we had the papal colours. She had the words *An Rinn agus An Sean Phobal* in Irish letters emblazoned in yellow in the centre. We were all going to see Pope John Paul II say Mass in Galway.

In our excitement we had eaten our sandwiches by the time we drove into Clonmel. When the priest took his packed sandwiches out around Limerick, we noted the neatly packed, delicious-looking contents of his lunch box – the leg of a chicken, the ham sandwiches and two little queen cakes. We watched ravenously as he ate every mouthful, hoping he might offer us some, but of course he felt no such inclination.

We were bone-tired by the time we got to Ballybrit. It was drizzling and damp. Once out of the minibus, we joined the hundreds of thousands and walked through mucky fields, guided by stewards until we were ushered into a corral. We were herded in with the Waterford and Lismore diocese to either lean against the rough wooden fencing that had been put in place or sit on the ground.

The Pope's Visit

The sky was grey, laden with rain, but the helicopters that flew over again and again and the warm-up acts kept us entertained. Bishop Eamonn Casey and Fr Michael Cleary kept the ball rolling, belting out chorus after chorus of 'By the Rivers of Babylon' and 'Totus Tuus' until the music began to swell and the voices of some 280,000 were finally unleashed. Some of us slept until the main event, leaning on the wooden fencing or lying on our raincoats in between the mucky shoes and boots that trampled around us. Each delegation must have been clearly visible that day, stretching out across the field with a huge panoply of waving flags and white faces looking up to see the pope.

Hours seemed to slip by until the main event began and we saw the man himself emerge onto the stage. He blessed us and waved through the mist. His vestments were blown all around him but his charisma kept us mesmerised.

In hindsight I recall his all-embracing proclamation of 'Young People of Ireland, I love you!' He delivered it in that characteristically strong Polish accent and I realise that it must have come straight from his heart, bursting from him spontaneously in response to our youth, our innocence and our warm welcome. When he said, 'Moladh go deo le Dia' – *praise be to God forever* – us Gaelgóirí from Ring felt he was talking directly to us and we were completely smitten. We cheered him on and laughed at the lovely guttural effort he had made, roaring our approval with everyone else, applauding him when he smiled at the sea of drenched faces. There he was, a real man on a dais, and he had travelled to be with us.

For months and even years afterwards, those two phrases – his Polish intonation intact – were often invoked, either at the top of the steps into our sitting room or at the table in our kitchen. 'Moladh go deo le Dia' or 'Young People of Ireland I love you'. Although we spoke them in jest at such times, they were also uttered in fond remembrance of Pope John Paul's style and personality.

The cold is uppermost in my mind as I think back to that outdoor Mass in Galway when there were seventy-seven robed figures concelebrating together at the distant altar. We followed their marionette-like movements. The Mass seemed to happen like a pantomime at times. Prayers and blessings over the bread and wine were blown away on the wind, while we shivered and watched and the mute show continued, only punctuated a couple of times when the wind carried back an odd line or two.

And on that day in Galway, we waved our banner, swaying to the strains of the hymns, and the creeping cynicism that had been settling into my brain and my person was washed away – for a time, at least. It was the embarrassing but exquisitely irresistible urge to weep that I remember too. I allowed tears to stream down my cheeks along with the thousands of others who were there when we sang 'Totus Tuus' and 'Ag Críost an Síol'. And as happens after all the best outings of one's youth, when we trudged back to the minibus we joined a long queue of buses and headed for home, tired but sated.

32

Nana Mouskouri

There was a year in the seventies when Nana Mouskouri was famous around the world and we knew all of her songs. I used to sing the one about Little Jimmy Brown who lived in the mountains high above the valley. I sang it when I was called up to the mike at the top of the bus once as we wound our way home. We'd left the Presentation school gates early in the morning on a school trip to Kilkenny Castle and Dunmore Cave.

My sister Miriam used to join in at the chorus and do the tolling bell as it marks out the stages of Little Jimmy Brown's life. So she bonged away musically at the precise moments from her seat on the bus. Bong! Bong! she sang, until Mrs Radley, not understanding the significance of her *a cappella* singing, frowned and signalled energetically for her to stop. Blushing with embarrassment, Miriam clammed up like a crab, shot dagger-looks at our geography teacher and I sang on like a diva.

When summer rolled in we became familiar with Nana Mouskouri's famous dark brown, shoulder-length, centrally-parted and perfectly coiffed hair, as well as her thick black glasses, her kaftans, her strong Greek accent and her rural background. I learned how she was first discovered. It seemed she was at home helping in the kitchen in her village, singing her heart out, when a passing record producer overheard her magnificent voice. It must have sailed out softly through an open window on the evening breeze, stopping him in his tracks. Immediately, the story went, he went in to meet this virtuoso and offered to make her a star.

The story of Nana's discovery while singing in her mother's kitchen struck a personal chord with me. It seemed magical and yet possible to me, especially when I was doing the washing up or hoovering and feeling that my days were full of Cinderella-like drudgery. I wanted to sing my heart out and experience the dizzy heights of universal adulation and admiration. I dreamed of being asked for encore after encore.

There were skylights in all of the bedrooms in our house at home and those who passed along the road outside would pass underneath these windows. Although it was more usually frequented by Harty's cows swaying and pushing as they made their way home to the farm to be milked in the evening, I held out hope that one day someone would pass and discover me.

So, occasionally, when the hot days arrived and Grecian luck seemed abroad, the sky a blue dome with an odd cloud drifting by, I'd wander aimlessly upstairs to loll in my bedroom, organise my books and sing. Of course, I'd make sure the skylight was open. I'd sing softly at first in order to beguile any listeners who might be passing and then I would sing *molto fortissimo* to impress. At times I'd hum, so as to sound nonchalant and casual.

On those summer days when all things seem connected and the world was full of possibility, my voice swelled out through the skylight, trilling and rising on each crescendo. I sang a selection of songs by the McGarrigles such as 'Foolish You', 'The Summer I Went Swimming' and 'Heart Like a Wheel'. I sang 'Buachaill ón Éirne' and 'Sliabh Geal gCua', 'An Chúillfhionn' and 'An Goirtín Eornan'. I imagined the music dropping like a blessing onto the fuchsia bushes along the road outside. I heard the cows munching like a sweet counterpoint to my song and I was happy.

One day, my father came in to the kitchen to tell me I'd received a compliment. He told me that a neighbour on his way home the evening before had heard me singing through the skylight and that he'd stopped to listen. He'd been very impressed, my father said. 'He said you have a lovely voice.'

I felt unmasked by the compliment and I blushed to think of him standing underneath the skylight listening. The man who'd heard me only lived up the road from us and he was not my idea of a wand-waving impresario. I was not at all excited by the compliment from this dark-haired man with an easy way about him, who'd wander by our house, the hint of a gleam in his eye. Suddenly, it seemed too foolish to sing in my bedroom any more, waiting to be discovered. I vowed to sing in the kitchen from then on and to forget about the skylights upstairs. I vowed to sing for my mother and myself alone. And whether the window in the kitchen was open to the world or not, I would hardly care at all, at all …

33

Mario Lanzo

When we sang certain songs, my sisters and I turned into extravagant divas. In the back seat of the green Mini with my parents up front, we'd travel along, singing our lungs out, competing furiously for recognition. We'd warble away, jockeying quietly for the top slot. Often at the end of a performance, one of us might elbow the other and assert ownership in the deadliest of serious tones, 'That's my song!'

We loved Percy French for his melodious tunes and his brilliant story lines. 'Drumcolliher' was given a frequent outing in the back of the car, each of us taking a verse and joining in at the chorus.

The song 'Abdul Abulbul Amir' about a bold and brave soldier in the ranks of the Shah of Iran, who challenged a Russian soldier to a fight after he'd trod on his toe, always got us going, the martial beat stoking us up no end.

'A Mother's Wish' left the biggest lump in our throats. It was about an elderly couple at home on the farm by themselves, 'the auld man at the plough, with no grown up son nor daughter to help them carry on'. Our voices would catch at the loneliness of it and at the end we'd droop in exhaustion in the back of the car, unable to go on in the face of such misery.

We also loved Rolf Harris's song about the 'Two Little Boys' who played on their wooden horses until they grew up and went off to war. We loved the poignancy of their story, our voices catching again as it unfolded, especially when one of the boys lay dying. The image of Jack galloping away to where Joe lay wounded was enough to have us surreptitiously wiping away a shameful tear or two. When we sang 'Did you say, Joe, I'm all a-tremble, perhaps it's the battle's noise, but I think it's that I remember when we were two little boys', we'd ladle on the emotion and sing it a second time for good measure.

But it was Mario Lanza and his singing which helped us give voice to a wild exuberance that bubbled up inside of us, especially in our teenage years. The dark-haired Italian-American tenor had a place in our hearts partly because he had a great look of our father but also because we knew that our Aunt Máire, who was Sr Alphonsus and the principal of a school in Rome, taught his daughters.

Even doing housework, if his record was playing it was hard to resist the urge to waltz across the floor: the upright polisher with a mind of its own would twirl like a psychotic dance partner beside us and we'd sing like sirens.

At home in Ring one Saturday, our parents had to leave us two older ones alone for a night. As we waved them off, an unaccustomed feeling of possibility took hold of us and a party seemed like the perfect way to celebrate our freedom. I was about sixteen years of age at the time. We invited a few friends who were on holiday nearby and we waited with a growing sense of excitement, hoping we might even lure some boys along as the friends had brothers! As payment for minding the shop for Dada we helped ourselves to bags of Tayto and bottles of Keane's OK Orange.

Girls, all girls, duly arrived. We noted that they came without their brothers but it didn't matter once the record player was set to play and Mario Lanza's rich voice was filling the room in no time. *Drink, drink, drink, to lips that are red and sweet as the fruit on the tree,* he sang. *Drink, Drink, Drink.* The beat took hold of us and we began to twirl around the room, waltzing in circles, taking partners, crashing into chairs. Our dog, Jingle, tried to join in, barking and jumping with us as we sang along to the chorus. The rising chords, lifting towards a tumultuous, re-petitious crashing of *Drink, Drink, Drink, let the toast start, may young hearts never part! Drink, Drink, Drink,* it had us swirling in ever faster circles. It was freeing and exhilarating. We threw caution to the wind and laughed, drunk on the fun of it.

It was then I noticed a pair of watchful eyes peering in at us through the window. There was no sound, just a grey face, gaunt and still, monitoring our every move. Hannie's arrival sent a shiver down my back. Our elderly neighbour from across the road, who had been asked to keep an eye on us, stood motionless at the window until we all came to a stop. Each of us turned to face those piercing eyes burning into us like gimlets. She never said a word. She just waited until we were still and Mario Lanza's voice had been silenced. Then she turned and limped away slowly towards her house.

I watched her go, my heart beating madly. She stopped when she had reached the gate and looking back, she shook her head from side to side as if in bemusement. The party petered out after that and our friends went home.

After everyone had gone, our hearts were still beating furi-ously; we sat quietly on the couch, not daring to put the turn-table on again. We could still hear the voice of Mario Lanza swirling in our heads, however, banishing the blues. Miriam and I smiled at each other conspiratorially as the music swelled.

My father with me as a baby, standing on the breakwater in Passage East on New Year's Day 1960.

Me, RoseAnn (*seated*) and Miriam, full of beans, at Lower Newtown.

Mama with me as Little Red
Riding Hood at Geneva Barracks.

Me (*third from right, front row*) in second babies at St John of God National
School on Passage Road, Waterford.

In my First Holy Communion dress, with Miriam (*standing*), RoseAnn and our mother, as photographed by Annie Brophy.

The three of us at Scoil Náisiúnta na Rinne in the early 1970s.

Having a picnic with Dada.

Me at boarding school in Cork when boarders sometimes got up on the roof.

At home on the garden seat with my father, Jingle at our feet.

In search of our
Martell relatives in
Corsica.

Relaxing with Mama after hanging her paintings for an
art exhibition in An Rinn.

Dada and me at home on the couch.

Enjoying the sun at home – me, Mama and RoseAnn.

RoseAnn and myself supporting the Waterford hurlers.

My mother and myself at the White Horses restaurant in Ardmore.

Me on Ceann a Bhathla in Ring.

34

A Gentleman Caller

We used to call him Dripsey in primary school. It was an affectionate nickname but, thinking back, I'm not sure if he liked it or not. (I was never clear about how he got his nickname but I know that it had something to do with feeding a calf when he was small.) His real name was Marcus. Imagine my surprise when he knocked at our front door in Baile na nGall one summer's evening.

I was now a student at university in Cork – where I was studying for a Bachelor of Arts degree in English and Irish – but was at home on holidays at the time of his visit. My father was busy making a couple of new lobster pots in one corner. He looked up and greeted Dripsey in Irish. 'Dia's Muire duit,' he said.

In school, in *rang a sé* (sixth class), I remembered how he used to sit in front of me and another girl and how he would twirl around, full of mock outrage, when we tried to write on the back of his neck with a biro, or how he'd leap up like a scalded cat when we dug the tip of a compass into his backside. We were full of devilment sitting in the back row. We loved annoying Dripsey because he'd react and pretend to be cross. He had an infectious laugh and we loved making him squeal.

Dripsey answered my father's greeting and wove his way unsteadily into the room – his unsteadiness making me realise that he was most likely on his way home from the pub. As he came closer, I noticed how he had the same freckles and feathery-light red hair of his youth.

'This is Marcus,' I said introducing him to my mother who was sitting in her armchair, her legs tucked under her, knitting away. She smiled at Marcus and glanced briefly at me. I saw her curiosity and her enjoyment of my confusion at the unexpected appearance of Dripsey. I could see what both my parents were thinking: how interesting, here's a suitor come to call on our daughter.

It felt awkward but I invited him to sit down. He took a seat and sat up straight as best he could. He took a moment to take stock of the room and the three of us. I sat back into my seat in the fourth corner and took up the dress I had been altering. We were a hive of industry. Dripsey swallowed nervously.

We had no television or radio on – all three of us too consumed in our work to think of such distractions. Evening time, before night fell, was always a period of great activity and creativity in our house. While it was still bright and balmy outside, my parents would beaver away in the garden or the kitchen, digging or cooking, carving or painting until the light was gone and the creative urge was spent.

My father put his pots down for a moment to chat with Dripsey, who seemed to be struck dumb. I saw a blush of embarrassment spread across his face. Dripsey smiled but it was as if the confidence that had carried him up to our front door had suddenly deserted him and he found himself tongue-tied and alone in a room full of strangers. In his presence I heard the hum of activity in the room. It was almost deafening. I just nodded at him, not knowing what to say.

'I'm sewing in a zip,' I offered. He smiled shyly but was clearly none the wiser.

A Gentleman Caller

I saw him looking at a piece of driftwood that my mother had hanging on the wall over the piano. My father always said the piece looked like a fellow leaning against a wall about to relieve himself. Our walls were full of such items – pieces of driftwood, paintings, shells, plates and photographs. Dripsey's eyes squinted as his gaze fell on one of my mother's shell pictures.

'Dada's making a new line of lobster pots,' I told him. He scratched his head and the minutes ticked on. I suppose I didn't make it much easier for him. Nor did I explain how the instinct to make things took hold of us when the rooms were filled with the luminous orange light of the dying sun, just before it falls below the skyline behind Dungarvan.

Dripsey laughed nervously.

'It's like the ICA,' he said. We laughed at his observation, knowing he had us down to a T and that he had hit the nail on the head when he compared us to the Irish Countrywomen's Association. Despite this, I was not amused by his unannounced appearance – even when he gave me a hangdog look, my expression was condescending.

Inside, though, I did feel some pity. I saw the little boy in his merry eyes and I knew he was unmanned and that he'd come on a fool's errand. He stayed for a minute or two more and then he made to go. It was the effort of standing up from the moving armchair that nearly overwhelmed him. I didn't go to help him, not wanting to embarrass him further. Or was it that my heart had hardened? As he passed by me, I noticed how pale he was. And part of me wanted him to stay. He was only a young man, after all, my own gentleman caller.

He nodded goodbye to my mother and father. He took in the room again with one last look. I smiled as I waved him off and thanked him for calling. The ring of Guinness around his mouth curled into a sort of a crumbled ellipse when he smiled. Then he walked off into the evening. And I knew for certain that he'd never call again.

35

The Helvick Summer

My father and I made for an ungainly pair walking down to the pier in our oilskins in the mornings that summer, staggering under the weight of all the gear that we carried. We had to manage the oars, the spurs, the fish box, a bucket of bait, a life-jacket, the petrol tank, two knives, rope and a few other odds and ends. Sometimes my mother would run us down in the car, but mostly we walked down by ourselves.

Fishing with your father sounds like a good idea. It was, but mostly we lost out on the fun and fished in silence. I'd wait stony-faced while he started the engine.

'Tarraing an téad sin isteach,' he'd say – *pull that rope in* – making his way down to show me how it was done. I hated being shown what to do. I'd sit in the bow, sometimes toying with the notion of slipping over the gunnel into the waves.

My father was always a thoughtful man with a great sense of fun. He could tell a story and you'd be smiling in no time if you were in his company. He was good with people, but with me – that summer, at least – he was at a loss.

I was a twenty-year-old college student who'd come home to fish for lobsters. Many of my friends were travelling to Germany or Denmark that summer to find work in hotels, or building sites or in bars, but I thought I'd stay home and earn money fishing with my father. The idea had appealed to me, at first. But the lobsters were scarce and the weather wasn't great and I began to resent both the work and being at home. All summer we fished and if I opened my mouth at all it was usually to argue with my father.

Once loaded and in the boat, he'd begin to pull in the anchor and start pumping juice into the engine. I had my own jobs, but he was always nervous of me in the boat. He sat and steered from the stern, worried in case we'd run aground or capsize in a freak wave.

The engine did cut out on us one day. We'd just dropped a line of sixteen pots. He pulled the starter again and again as we bobbed up and down in the swell but the engine died with each tug.

'We'll have to row back,' he said, worried about getting too close to the rocks. 'Will you be able?'

'Of course, come on,' I said pulling an oar out, almost losing it in the waves with the effort. We exhausted ourselves rowing until we finally rounded the pier into Helvick. It was only when we'd rested that my father realised that the petrol tank was empty and only in need of a refill from the spare gallon that he always carried on board!

The weather was bad all that summer in keeping with my mood, which was mostly dark and sullen. But still we had a handful of beautiful days when we'd haul in the lobster pots out near the cliffs with the sun glinting off the green water. It was a bonus if there was a lobster in the pot when we pulled it out of the sea. We'd both smile then, relishing the excitement as water cascaded from the mesh.

'That's a fine one, just the right size,' he'd say. 'The bit of sun makes all the difference. If we had another few days like this we'd make a good few bob, what do you think, Katie? Will we come out this evening for a few mackerel? We might fill the box.' I'd give him a nod and he'd continue, 'Do you know, if a fellow had a bigger boat he could make a fortune.'

The idea of spending my holidays getting a tan, pulling pots like a Greek fisherman and lolling around the pier with the locals had initially appealed to me. But my hands were soon cut and rough. My feet slithered about in an old pair of loose runners, squishing away as I moved about the boat. My hair, which was closely cropped, became matted and sticky from the spray. I stopped washing it altogether.

Shuffling down in the cold grey to a deserted pier at half seven in the morning to catch the tide is no fun. As the days passed my scowl deepened. I wore a faded sweatshirt and a pair of dirty jeans cut off at the knees. I was deeply unhappy, convinced that I was a shapeless, insignificant lump without any redeeming features. As we pulled up to the pier one day, two fishermen came over to lend a hand as we docked alongside their trawler.

'Throw that line up here like a good young man,' one of them shouted down to me. It was all the confirmation I needed. I'd been called a young man and no one had even batted an eyelid! A few days later, as I walked out of the ladies' toilets on the pier, a woman stared at me, doing a double take as she looked from me to the *Mná* sign on the doorway overhead.

We spent our nights in the kitchen while the midges outside pitted themselves against the lighted window. Dada washed his supper down with a drink of Guinness. He and Mama chatted while I gorged myself on crab claws, bread and cheese. I felt myself expand, my stomach swelling and my bottom spreading into my thighs.

The lobsters were scarce. We caught fewer and fewer each week. When we did, I had to put rubber bands around their pinchers to stop them from fighting. You'd hear them clacking away as we lowered the box into the water where we kept them alive until the dealer came to buy them once a week.

It was bright and crystal clear out beyond the headland the day I stabbed the conger eel. We were heaving the pots up from the seabed and were nearing the last one.

I shivered involuntarily when I saw him trapped in one of the pots. His long body, as thick as a man's arm, moved about, slithering slowly inside. His jaws opened wide as he twisted himself about and tried to bite down on the plastic-covered wire mesh. I tried to manoeuvre him out through the neck of the trap, turning it upside down. Finally he fell out heavily onto the boards. He tried to squirm away and he had almost made it under the board to the belly of the bilge underneath but I hunched down and stuck the knife into his head. He eyeballed me with two black, steady eyes. I hoisted him up onto the thwart and held the blade steady as he tried to twist away. His strength travelled up my arm like a current. I gritted my teeth at the crunching sounds his bones made against the blade and I felt like a murderer. Still, I held the knife steady and I savoured the kill.

I should have kept him for bait. I should have cut him up and thrown the pieces in the bucket but I wasn't thinking of practicalities like that. I only wanted to get rid of him and so, with a great effort, I lifted him up on the hilt of the knife and heaved him over the side. He slipped over the gunnel and into the water. I saw him sink slowly underneath us. It was as if my own blackness and confusion slipped away down with him.

As he disappeared, my poor summer mood lifted and I slowly began to feel exultant. The spray soaked us as we travelled home on the tide that day. I smiled and looked ahead, bracing myself for another soaking. We looked in towards shore and I saw the cars driving along the road into Dungarvan. They were only landlubbers, not hunters of the deep like us.

I asked my father if he wanted to go out fishing for mackerel that evening. We headed off after tea. We shouted to the others who were dropping lines close by: 'Are ye catching many?' 'Is the buyer coming tonight?' 'Nach bhfuil se go deas anois?' *Isn't it nice now?*

Mackerel were breaking the surface in silvery flashes all around. Seagulls were screeching and swooping as I pulled in six mackerel at a time on my line. They danced sharp jigs on the boards before they lay still. The sun's orange light steeped the whole place in fire before it began to sink behind the Knockmealdown Mountains.

'Isn't it lovely now?' my father said.

'It is,' I agreed and I asked him then if he'd seen the eel I'd killed earlier in the day.

'No. Did you keep him for bait?' he wondered.

'I did not,' I told him, disappointed that I hadn't thought of it myself.

'Was he big?'

'He was a monster, I could hardly lift him up on the knife … you wouldn't have kept him yourself for bait.'

'I don't know what we'll do with you at all,' he said laughing and I had to smile as the two of us pulled in our lines and headed back.

It was near the end of the summer and I was soon heading

back to university in Cork. My father was sad to finish. Pulling pots absorbed him completely.

That was years ago. Years later over a drink we'd recall the summer we had spent fishing for lobsters and we'd smile at the memory of it all. It's only now I know that it was a summer we would never have again.

36

Tribal Dance

Passers-by in Cork city grew used to hearing our screams and raised voices, our loud music and banging doors. We lived in a house on Hartland's Avenue, which was not far from the UCC campus. No neighbours panicked when black smoke issued from our windows after we'd set the chimney on fire. They knew we were students.

Steam used to hit the cold surfaces and run in rivulets of condensation down the walls and windowpanes, giving our little rented house the feel of a hammam.

Those days of lectures, library assignations and lounging over coffees in the restaurant were also full of squabbles, flounces, bitter feuds and burnt toast. In our house, we lived on tea and All-Bran, and we spent our time counting calories, dieting and weighing ourselves. There was usually an air of upheaval in that rented bungalow, which I shared with four other girls. We were all like aliens from outer space who'd landed in Cork. I was from a Gaeltacht; the others came from such far-flung planets as Tralee in County Kerry, Kanturk in County Cork, Birr in County Offaly and Waterford city.

It was a new world to us and though we came from different schools and different counties we clung together like sheep, nervously stepping out and forward as a group, learning how to act like grown-ups. We'd become friends in our first year at university when we'd stayed in La Retraite Hostel, where we each had our own room and regular meals. When we began our second year we found this house on Hartland's Avenue that we rented together and stayed in until the end of university.

Clothes were borrowed, books were lost, dinners were sometimes forgotten and lectures were missed as our house echoed with the sound of our names – Ana, Kay, Maria, Máire and Catherine.

Outside our house there was a small garden of weeds, a lush wilderness of knee-high grass interspersed with yellow dandelions and dandelion clocks. A lone monkey puzzle tree stood stark and pointless in their midst.

We lived for the moment when a handsome, dashing, dangerous rake would fall in love with one of us and whisk us off our feet. We spent our days talking about the elusive young men we had spotted crossing the university's quadrangle. We were only interested in the unavailable ones, of course, and they provided a topic of endless conversation for us. We gave them nicknames so we could discuss them at length without fear of discovery. The Ruler was duly christened after an encounter with one of our number when he'd reached across a library desk and asked for the loan of a ruler. We came to know another student as The Cow after we spotted him drinking a full pint of milk in one go outside the college restaurant. Brown Jumper was Brown Jumper because he seemed to have only the one and wore it constantly. The boy who was Casper was so because he was quiet and a lot like the fictional cartoon character Casper, the Friendly Ghost. It was The Eagle's strong profile that earned him his name.

Each of these individuals was particularly important to us and each sighting had to be analysed by all of us. Did The Ruler say anything when you passed him? What exactly did he say? What was The Cow wearing? What was he carrying? Would you say The Eagle was going home for the weekend?

We tried to keep a check on their whereabouts by keeping their comings and goings under constant observation. We were the original stalkers, waiting at corners to see them emerge from lectures. We took up seats behind them in the reading rooms where they studied so that we could maintain round-the-clock surveillance. In case subterfuge was called for we'd always have books open in front of us and so we gave the impression we were studying. To survey all approaches to the quadrangle outside we'd pay regular visits to the on-campus ladies toilets.

Of course we had plenty of male friends but these were not the ones who set our pulses racing. These were the ones we treated dismissively and derisively and who still came back for more. They visited us late in Hartland's Avenue, hoping to cadge a cup of tea. They bought us flowers, they treated us to coffee in the restaurant and they quoted lines from Bob Dylan. But these were not the stuff of exquisite ecstasy; we were looking for the grand romance and that most elusive of impossible emotions – love.

Then, one night, a number of the young men on whom all our attention was focused descended on us in our bungalow. That night went down in history as a visit of almost magical proportions. As they rapped on the glass panels of our front door, one of us was emerging from the bathroom after a bath. In they trooped, these young men. Emboldened by alcohol, they seemed to swagger in. And the larger than life presence of such attractive males – those who had stoked our imaginations over many months – suddenly being in our midst left us excited and borderline hysterical. They came in like marauding Vikings, full of devilment and mayhem. They responded to our panicked shrieks with great gusto when we ran from them – running as if we were about to be ravished. It was tremendous fun.

The images I have of the rest of that night are like a dream sequence now. With steam emerging from the bathroom, the smell of talc in the air and the general aura of bathing wafting through the house, some of them decided to strip. Once naked, these mischievous interlopers rampaged through our nunnery of domesticity. Like some tribal dance troupe, they made quick sorties into our rooms, swinging their hips. At one point they shook clouds of Johnson's Baby powder over us.

When they left we remained alert, thrilling from the experience. There had been no physical contact but the veil of illusion had been torn aside. Ever after that adult romp, us girls felt we'd grown up. We'd lived through an experience that no child would understand. We were no longer innocents. We'd seen male nakedness. We'd experienced a night of wild exuberance, abandon and hilarity. When they left, we were exhausted but thrilled. After that the chase for each of us to know one of these male students intimately was on in earnest.

37

Finals

We'd borrow different jeans and tops from each other's drawers, taking care and time each day in our preparations before our ascent from Hartland's Avenue to the lofty plains of UCC. We'd stand up on a chair in the sitting room in front of a mirror that hung over an empty fireplace and, turning this way and that, we'd check how we looked from behind.

After attaining just the right look – and with a final smear of Vaseline across our lips – we'd gather up our belongings, don a Levi's jacket or a duffel coat and sashay our way down to the campus to spend the day watching out for boys.

Throughout the day we starved ourselves until dinner time in the evening. Instead of food, we'd talk over coffee at elevenses and lunchtime about how much weight we'd gain if we had an apple, a banana, a slice of toast, a carton of yoghurt or a bowl of All-Bran. In the evening we'd trudge back to our house for dinner as prepared by one of us – peanuts in squid ink was one I recall that Máire prepared that did not go down too well. Better days included bacon and cabbage, pork chops and fried onions, and a well-known Tralee dish as prepared by our Kerry representative, Kay, was a tasty stew-like affair called 'skirts and kidneys'.

As the days progressed over the course of a week, you'd find us counting the dwindling amount of pennies that we'd left in our house kitty – to which we contributed five pounds each every week. I used to buy the potatoes and cabbage from a vegetable shop on Barrack Street. I remember the long trek uphill to our house after purchasing the various ingredients. I'd buy the meat from a butcher on my way home. My culinary skills amounted to boiling the lot to bally-rags and dishing it up, steaming and hot onto the plates. I was able to make white onion sauce but this was an optional extra and did not always appear. We'd devour the lot in a couple of minutes.

When we had gorged and eaten our fill we'd retire to the sitting room, lie on the couch or the hearthrug or the floor and discuss the perfectly reasonable habit the ancient Romans had of visiting the vomitorium. (I realise now how we diced with danger and put our health at risk but we were not averse to a spot of bulimia, not to mention a touch of anorexia, often congratulating ourselves on our combined willpower in not eating.)

No one could ever have accused us of being academic. Although we basked in the glorious stereotype of the lofty, idealistic student who spends her life reading, writing essays, attending lectures and tutorials, studying literature or science and thinking great thoughts, we were far from that. It's a wonder I knew where the library was.

When exam time came around, dinners became a distant memory. One sunny evening, it struck me how ill-prepared I was to sit my upcoming final exams. I phoned home and poured out my worries to my mother. Panic-stricken I cried like a baby as I realised the ignominy of failure that awaited me. I continued to blubber until I finally said goodnight to my demented mother and father, reassuring them that I'd be all right, leaving them in no doubt that I'd probably have to be fished out of the Lough – a lake near campus – but that they were not to worry.

Some hours later, my spirits restored by a walk around the

said Lough, I was surprised to see my mother drive along. She had come to support me and give me confidence in my hour of need. I berated her for coming and treating me like a little schoolgirl. But stay she did for a couple of days to pet me and drive me to the Maltings, the former flour mill and malting buildings which had been converted for use by the university into exam and lecture halls. She left me there in the mornings on time for my exams. In the evenings she picked me up, cooked me dinner, gave me fortifying Guinness and talked me up to a position of power.

It was during one of the nights my mother was with us that Johnny D – a love-lorn young man and fellow student from north Cork – staggered up to our front door to pledge his troth. He was not on our lust list but he was a friend and a regular visitor to our house. It was very late and we were all asleep inside. Peace reigned; the house was in darkness. Perhaps the fact that my mother was staying with us on that particular night had something to do with the tender domesticity of our slumber. All was calm until the sounds of soft fumblings right outside Ana's window woke her.

Johnny D was in love with each of us. Full of ardour and a determination to gain admittance he wanted to pledge his heart and even his soul to one of us. He'd crept up to the nearest bay window, tripping over the dandelions in his way and had tried to peer in. Fortified with pints, he was ready to make the depth of his feelings known to one of us. It didn't matter which one. Ana heard him and, petrified, rose and ran across the hall into my bedroom.

Soon we were all awake, rising like ghosts in the semi-darkness. We huddled together in a bedroom, our voluminous nightdresses reminiscent of the Brontë sisters themselves, our fear keeping us mute. Unaware who the knocker was at this point, we had no idea what to do.

We looked to my petite mother for guidance and she was more than equal to the challenge. Straightening up, all five feet of her, she cast any hint of timidity aside and with no one to protect her she marched towards the offending disturbance outside the bedroom window and pulled back the curtain.

Poor Johnny D didn't stand a chance. He staggered back when my mother was revealed to him. 'Go away,' she warned him, 'or I'll call the guards.'

We girls drew breath in unison, impressed yet fearful. We peered out through the glass and saw the shadowy figure outside backing away sheepishly, an air of confusion about him. He seemed to be wondering if he'd called to the wrong house or if he might be suffering from some queer hallucinogenic vision. We saw him trip over the roots of the monkey-puzzle near our gate. It was then we recognised him as none other than our friend Johnny D.

Full of renewed confidence, the next day I waved my mother off. In the end, I was glad she had come to my rescue. She'd injected new energy and hope into my flagging spirit. Later, when we girls passed Johnny D on the street we waved happily to him. He waved back cautiously, looking confused as he passed. We never mentioned his late night call. We had other fish to fry, now that our final academic year was nearly over.

With adulthood beckoning me on in earnest, I began to think about joining the work force. To that end, I'd have to find a teaching job I realised, and so I braced myself and set out to face the great wide world.

The Great Wide World

38

My First Interview

Some weeks ago I came across a few dog-eared pages on Blue Basildon Bond paper covered in my own youthful writing. It was an account I had written of my first adult job interview a long time ago in Kilkenny. I read it and the memory of when my younger self had applied for different teaching jobs slowly returned.

Reading this material was like meeting a separate version of me, a person who was familiar but completely forgotten. I read with wonder to know what I had been like at twenty-one. The writing was crystal clear and spikey. The first two pages were written in ink with a fountain pen and after running dry I continued in Biro for the last two. My punctuation is all there, with a liberal sprinkling of exclamation and question marks.

I described how I left home that morning at 9.30 a.m., my mother standing at the door to wave me off. I was thumbing to town because our car was out of action. Dressed in my mother's suit, I walked behind Sean Harty's cows until they turned off into a field. I continued straight on along the road, my canvas bag bulging with a balled up mack and a scarf in case it rained, a pair of high-heeled sandals for the interview and a jumper to change into afterwards.

From Dungarvan I took the bus. CIÉ Express: two pounds. No return fare for students. When we pulled into Plunkett Station in Kilkenny, I got off the bus and with all my hurrying bumped into a little girl. 'Mind the lady,' her mother said. *Me*, I have written with a question mark, *a lady?*

Yes, I remember that incident now and how grown-up I felt in the beige-belted suit. How I smiled to myself because I felt sophisticated, like my mother, or like an adult in a film. I also remember how I slid on a slab of stone on my way out of the station and how the jolt of it almost caused me to lose my balance. The near-fall made me nervous and caused a lump to form in my throat as I walked towards my interview.

I reached the county hall without any more complications and I made my way up to the ninth floor. I write that the elevator's upward surge didn't help to calm me down. *Sitting on her own at the end of the corridor was another Powlett-Jones*, I wrote. This was the character in a television series, which was about a shell-shocked young man's first teaching job after serving in the trenches during the First World War.

I joined this other candidate, who was also all decked out for the interview. I describe how she wore flesh-coloured tights, whereas my legs were bare. I was in a quandary as to whether I should go away and change into the pair of tights which were in my bag. *No*, I reasoned. *Be yourself.*

That decision may make or break me, I wrote. The intensity and seriousness of my youth rings like a bell with me today and I can only smile.

I sat and listened to the clock tick away and also furtively studied the girl beside me. She had a neat little black bag. *This one has it all going for her*, I wrote. And I recall the sensation of looking down at myself in desperation. On top of everything my skirt was buttoned up the front, which meant that when I crossed my legs my knees could be seen. I knew that whatever else happened I had to keep them covered in the interview.

Then I wrote that a fellow I knew from my Irish lectures in college, Tadhg, came out from his interview and the girl in the tights went in. He had had a haircut since I last saw him and minus his wiry, shoulder-length hair he looked smarter and cleaner than usual. *This is going to be tougher than I thought.*

I crossed my knees and pulled the slit closed. 'How many are in there?' I asked him.

'Three,' he responded.

Tadhg stayed chatting for a few minutes. He seemed relaxed after the interview and in no hurry to go. In due course the girl came out. She and Tadhg wished me luck as they backed away. I imagined they both looked pale. It was near dinner time. Hungry, I supposed. I wonder where Tadhg is now and if he is still teaching. Is he bald? He had very bright eyes and he was from Kerry.

Before I had time to gather myself again, one of the three interviewers came out and asked me my name. He went in again. Then he came back to the door and called me in.

Inside, the three interviewers sat in front of me at a table. I sat down opposite them, delighted because the table hid my knees and my old sandals, which I hadn't changed. So I relaxed and smiled across the table at them. I was ready. One fellow had a bushy beard, I noticed.

After half an hour they thanked me and I thanked them. I wasn't sure whether I had been dismissed or not so I said slán and with my documents in hand I made for the door.

That's all I wrote all those years ago.

The memories of those years are slipping back into my conscious memory now. I had forgotten how my mother always got up when I was leaving for interviews to get my breakfast, iron my blouse and wave me off. Our neighbour Sean Harty died some years ago and his cows no longer pass our house on their way up the hill to be milked. We miss the sound of their hooves on the cement shoulder and Sean's hup-hup as he followed them up the road. We miss the splashing of their runny brown dung as it plopped onto the stones and the shuffling of their bodies as they swayed and pushed against each other going up the road. The milking parlour is gone and there are new houses on the hill where we used to hear them bellowing during the night.

I don't know why I wrote an account of that morning. It was years before I had anything published. But finding it more than twenty years later has given me pause to remember that fresh green morning and I'm really glad I put that handwritten account in an old shoe box at the back of a wardrobe, where it remained, waiting for me to find it again many years later.

39

The Boys of 2F

I was short-listed for that job in Kilkenny in the early 1980s but before I knew it, I was offered a permanent job in the vocational school of Tipperary town, a role I accepted. It was my first teaching job, so I was very excited and eager to start.

From the beginning they could see I hadn't a clue. And I could see that those boys in 2F would try me sorely. They were a mix of farm and town boys. Some of them came on the bus each morning and some were often late, wandering in as if they were still only waking up. A handful of them were bright-eyed and thin. I remember them pouring into my classroom, whooping and hollering, hurling bags across the desks to a chorus of 'Well, Miss' and 'How are ye, Miss'. They were a ramshackle bunch of misfits. They all struggled in school – many of them were hardly able to read – and yet each one was as gifted and as clever as you'd ever want a boy to be. They were the bottom-rung class of second year and were viewed by nearly one and all as near hopeless cases when it came to schoolwork.

Of course, they loved mitching school, especially on mart days when they could stand at corners and smoke, chat and spit like grown-up men. They loved action films, bad language, rude gestures, double entendres and free classes. It goes without saying that they hated school, but most especially they hated Irish.

'Ah, Miss,' they'd moan when I gave them homework. I

spent days on the past tense, *An Aimsir Chaite*, hoping they'd respond to the simplicity of speaking in this one tense. I tried to incite them to tell me what had happened to them – 'Cá raibh tú?' *Where were you?* 'Cad a tharla?' *What happened?* 'Inis dom faoi sin!' *Tell me about that.* I'd get them to repeat lines. In between they'd continue their whispered talk about Rambo and Arnold Schwarzenegger and whatever programmes they'd seen on television the night before. They also loved looking at wounds, gouging their names into the desks or onto their bags, and fighting and firing chalk at each other.

I taught them the Irish version of that lilting song, 'The Whistling Gypsy' and discovered that they especially loved the chorus, which they corrupted joyously to suit their own designs, rhyming 'do' with 'screw'. *Ah, dee do ah dee do da day.* The rude alternative corrupted the line entirely but at each chorus they'd sing that *Ah dee screw* section with renewed gusto and abandon, laughing and cheering themselves on, stamping and banging on the tables as we did a run-through for the recording that I was making.

It was only when I played back the tape that you could hear a pin drop as they listened to themselves in wonderment. It was a moment of discovery and wonder for me, too, as I realised that they wanted that – to be shown versions of themselves. It was like holding a mirror up to them and they were fascinated by what it revealed.

Day after day, they'd troop in and look up at me in anticipation of the recorder. It was as if they expected I was going to do a magic trick. 'A Bhuachaillí, tógaigí amach bhúr leabhair,' I'd say – *Boys, take your books out* – knowing I was a kind of commander-in-chief and that my job was to maintain order and reign in the troops when a skirmish broke out along the battlefront that was my classroom.

One Friday afternoon, when it was clear they only wanted to be away out the door and were only looking for an excuse to shout, jump out of their seats, tell a joke and run around the room, I brought two of them up to the top of the class to act out a make-believe exchange between a garda and a cyclist with no lights.

The seated boys showed no mercy as they egged on the two at the top, who did their best with the dialogue, blushing and stumbling over the words – until someone threw a pencil at the blackboard and the heckling and stomping gathered apace. I stormed up from the back of the classroom to try to restore order, the class at its most frenzied. Struggling to bring them under control, I looked about me wildly, wishing I could be beamed up. To my horror, I noticed one of the school's caretakers peering in through the door's glass panel. With his raised eyebrows and obvious shock, it was clear he disapproved of the chaos.

The day the inspector – aka the *cigire* – came, they did their best, whispering to each other to shut up, punching any neighbour who spoke out of turn. Their loyalty to me was never in question.

Today I miss those gentle if wild boys of Tipperary. And I feel great regard for them. I hope they are still laughing and sparring in the foothills of the Galtees. I hope they have work and I hope that on occasion they fill their lungs and sing 'The Whistling Gypsy', or 'An Spailpín Fánach' in Irish, complete with their own bawdy take on the lyrics.

40

Secrets of a Lost Diary

I recently came across an old diary I kept in the mid-1980s. My entries are cryptic. It's clear I was not a diligent or consistent diarist. There are short awkward bursts as I try to strike the right tone and experiment with words and style.

On Saturday 10 August 1985, I describe heading home to Ring from a day's shopping in Dublin with my sister: 'The train is crowded,' I wrote, 'people are standing. The sky is grey and it has rained a few times today. Poured! This country is getting more like Yugoslavia every day. Crows and nettles, rain and grime.'

I had obviously started to see the world at that stage!

It is the travelling element of life back then that surprises me most. In one entry I wrote that we went to Clonmel to shop for a dress for my mother who was going to a wedding. Halfway home we ran out of petrol. The forests were burning on the mountains and we could see the flames from the road, I wrote, obviously drawing strong parallels between my life and *War and Peace*.

In another entry I describe Miriam and I thumbing home from Cork, which was then about a two-hour journey. It seems it was a freezing, bitter day and it took us hours to get home. We hitched rides from eight different vehicles – all hyphenated with long waits in between. It seems we had been to a party in Ballincollig where I was heartless, giving a man in navy blue cords and a tight jumper a phoney phone number. *The jumper was pulled down to cover his pot belly and fat bottom*, I wrote: clearly the cruel objectivity and disinterest of my youth was fully intact.

Before I bought my first car it's clear that travelling by bus had been central to my life. In one entry, I describe a day we went to Dublin on the express intercity service. RoseAnn and I left at 7.45 a.m. and headed off on the three-hour journey zig-zagging along a winding secondary road, pulling in to stops in towns along the way. From Waterford we went to Thomastown and then Kilkenny. We slept on and off, trying to make ourselves comfortable in the upright seats. I recall an incident of someone suffering from a bout of travel sickness, which was a fairly common occurrence. In Carlow, the driver gave us a few minutes to dash in to 'powder our noses' and/or grab a cup of tea in a little coffee shop at the stop. We were stiff-legged by the time we pulled in again at another stop, in Castledermot, County Kildare, to leave out some passengers and get a chance to stretch our legs. It was here, in a pub, that the preserved arm of the strongest man in Ireland was on view in a dimly lit glass case.

As we entered Dublin, we sat up in our seats to take in the sights. Passing Heuston Station, the adrenaline started to pump and the combined effect of the traffic, the cyclists, the lorries and the olive green waters of the Liffey had us wiping clean the fogged-up windows, too exhilarated to be nonchalant any more. Crossing over O'Connell Bridge, we were pulling in to Busáras in no time and it was still only 11.05 a.m.

After that we walked up towards Henry Street and Arnotts. I remember how shopping was always a key part of those trips when we'd rifle through rails of clothes, jackets, tops and coats in the hope of spotting a bargain. I also list Grafton Street and Powerscourt as ports of destination. Then it was off for a rendezvous with Miriam, who was then studying in Dublin, and we had to drag ourselves away from all the boutiques, jewellery and shoe shops along the way to be in time for coffee in Wynn's Hotel.

I write that we couldn't stop laughing when Miriam un-wrapped our mother's tea braic, which we had carried with us. There and then she cut into it, making no attempt to hide her activity from the waiter who was leaning against the counter nearby, keeping a weather eye on us and our foosterings. It was coming up to teatime and getting dark outside when we said goodbye and made our way back to Busáras. I record that we got home that night at 9 p.m.

An entry from another day: back in Dublin, I describe the rain and a bus stop where I alighted amid people in transit, criss-cross lives that make patterns, infinite knots and tangles. Budding writer that I was, I added that it was futile to try to stop the zig-zag, make meaning or give structure to the hap-hazard effortless onward running trail of lives in the capital. Standing on the footpath I tell myself that I can dissolve into its orb or ricochet away.

As I return the diary to my bookshelf, I think that perhaps it's worth holding on to and that it's not time to toss it away just yet.

41

Praying in Prague

When I saw the little gold statue
locked behind glass,
a trapdoor
suddenly released
I fell down the years
to my gran and Passage East
with her rosary beads
and her devotion to the Child of Prague.*

Right beside the statue
I saw a framed picture of the Little Flower
and with that another
bolt came undone
and I tumbled through the tunnel of time
to my Auntie Gile
and her statues and her prayers to
St Thérèse of Lisieux – the Little Flower*
and the child of Prague.

Like a current,
The two women and their litanies ran through me.
Their big eyes,
full of beseeching and pleading,
took me back to then

Praying in Prague

when I was a child and a statue
was a focus in our lives.
When it stood in a place of pride
in Passage on a sideboard by the stairs.
And I saw my gran's lips move as she got down on her
   knees
And in Helvick years later, on my aunt's bedroom window
on a doily in the sun
I recalled the saint
framed by blue water all the way out to sea,
with our eyes lingering there on her little doll-size face.
The statue was a presence then,
to my child's eyes,
benign and calm,
it was the pulse in a corner
that directed heat into our hands.

That day in Prague,
a volt from the two of them,
their eyes large with longing
shot back up through me
when I knelt on the kneeler
in the little chapel
in front of the golden statue of the Child of Prague,
and the picture of the Little Flower.
I cried for the time that was gone
when prayers were directed
through a blessed prism heavenwards,
when back then it was to them, so clearly, an important
   ritual.

Their joint invocation
blew like a whistled breath.
As I remembered them long ago
I felt their lives rush through me,
whispering,
when I bowed my head to pray.

* This statue of the Infant Jesus, which is based in Prague, is referred to as the 'Child of Prague'. There was great devotion to this statue in Ireland all throughout the twentieth century. Many Irish households had their own nineteen-inch statue but the original Roman Catholic wooden wax-coated statue, which is studded with diamonds and decorated with a gold crown, resides in the Discalced Carmelite Church of Our Lady Victorious in Prague. Legends claim that the statue once belonged to Saint Teresa of Ávila of the Carmelite Order.

** St Thérèse of Lisieux – who was also known as the 'Little Flower' – was a Carmelite nun. She entered the convent in Lisieux in France at the age of fifteen. After a long struggle with tuberculosis, she died in 1897 at the age of twenty-four. The impact of *Story of a Soul*, a collection of her autobiographical manuscripts, printed and distributed a year after her death, was huge and as a result she became one of the most popular saints of the twentieth century. She was beatified in 1923 and canonised in 1925.

42

The Green Ray

I've spent evenings watching the sun sink into the sea in the hope of seeing that elusive green ray, that final splash of colour. It happens just before the sun dips into the ocean, the green rays of the sun remaining visible for a fraction longer than the red and orange rays. This green light phenomenon occurs when the dying rays are split into their separate parts by a sort of celestial prism, resulting in that final parting flash of green.

The green ray is mentioned in the 2007 film *Pirates of the Caribbean: At World's End* and J. R. R. Tolkien writes about the significance of the green flash in *The Hobbit*.

I first learned about the green ray, however, when I saw a French film by the great new wave director Eric Rohmer. *Le Rayon Vert* was screened in Trinity College in Dublin in the late 1980s. This was just after a turbulent time in my life, where – after four years – I'd decided to quit teaching and had moved to Dublin to pursue a career in journalism.

I loved the film's central character, Delphine, who is lonely and out of kilter with the world. She was about my own age at the time and she was living in an apartment on the Left Bank in Paris. I immediately identified with her and her uncertainty. As the story unfolds, the viewer is drawn to her more and more. She doesn't know what to do with herself in the city over the holidays. Her friends have decamped to the country and to cap it all her boyfriend has split up with her. She is invited to

Brittany to join friends but she can't settle there. She goes off to the Alps to be with other friends but she can't content herself there either. Then she tries Biarritz but, again, everyone seems to be happy and having fun except for Delphine.

The film, in truth, is about finding your path, about finding peace and purpose in life and in true cinematic fashion Delphine finally meets up with the man of her dreams, a fellow traveller, whom she accompanies on a walk along a cliff top to watch the sun go down. The romantic conclusion kept me enthralled, but I think there was also something about the film's metaphysical dimension that captivated me. In her travels, Delphine heard the story of the green ray as written by Jules Verne. He wrote that if you are lucky enough to see this ethereal light, you will know the truth that is in your own heart and in the heart of those near you. Naturally Delphine and her companion see the green ray together and immediately she knows what is in her heart and in the heart of the young man, and she knows peace.

'This ray has the virtue of making him who has seen it impossible to be deceived in matters of sentiment,' writes Jules Verne.

I remember walking home after the screening, trying to imagine what it would be like to know your own heart, as I surely would if I ever saw the green ray. When I came out of the auditorium it was a balmy sunny evening on Nassau Street and I was full of the possibilities of chance encounters and first love. It was the time of day when there is a pause in the evening; the point at which the end is nigh but the light just seems to hang there, waiting, as if the earth is savouring the last bit of heat from the sun. I listened to a ball striking the cricket bats on the lawns within Trinity and I remembered how James Joyce first spotted Nora Barnacle as she walked along the footpath on Nassau Street. I imagined how she must have looked when he saw her that day in June, with her rousse auburn hair and her free and elegant gait, her long skirts and her fine Galwegian eyes.

As I made my way home towards my flat in Sandymount, I half expected to see my own Joycean lookalike approach. With intense eyes, broad clothes-hanger shoulders and gallons of Gallic charm, I imagined him running up to ask if I'd enjoyed the film and if I'd like to go into the Mont Clare Hotel for some *vin rouge*. But I passed on into the darkening evening, going by Merrion Square and Northumberland Road, watching purply orange colours streak across the sky like lipstick. I held my breath as I went along: Nora, Delphine and I basking in the light, mystically connected by a story about the truth that's in the heart. I've never seen that luminously charged green ray. But one day, I expect I'll be surprised. I'm sure I will.

43

In a Train

The platform outside waits chill,
in the hum of its vacuum
people pass to and fro,
steps ricochet from dome to dome.

Penned in, we listen to the rustling settle.
We have windows and corner seats in which to huddle,
A clammy heat is just bearable,
but feet must not unfold or travel under any table;
tidy, they must remain quiet, like good children,
they must not fidget.
Elbows must not flap, eyes must not travel,
only covertly
to sneak bewildered glances at
women in ironed dresses, pearled, nail-varnished,
nyloned,
with a book or a magazine.
Ladies who look unconcerned and disdainful
and ever downwards except with a sigh
they might look up and with their ebbing breaths think –
how long more must I endure, I am worn out, my skin is
    creased
and, like dough, my glorious breasts lie jiggling on my
    swollen, solid belly.

In a Train

Like mice we sit
quiet,
with shiny beady, dull eyes,
but nothing to suggest the sprinkling and drenching
    rawness of every other day.

The land lies telling us secrets,
we don't slow down,
the tractor churns the clay and puffs
and we speed by.
Resting cows that ignore us,
draped on green, thinking.
They have their own lives to live.
They ponder and remain
gloriously flaccid.
A man on a chimney, a man that stands out, up against
    the grey sky,
unique, erect,
where are the chimney-climbers on this train?

44

The Two Germans

They were both very tall and very handsome. In fact, they looked as if they'd stepped out of a fashion magazine. One was called Christian and the other Heinrich. They were university students in Germany, soft spoken and gentlemanly. They explained that they were from Bavaria and I remember asking them if they were able to ski. Oh yes, they gushed; they skied every winter.

My friend Máire introduced me to them. We were all there together in Edinburgh. I had just finished a course in journalism in Dublin and I was on holidays visiting Máire, who was working at the university. They may as well have stepped out of the pages of a Mills & Boon story. These men were so like film stars that I hardly spoke to them for the duration of my stay. Saying that, they were friendly and open. I learned that they would be conscripted into the navy on their return to Germany and that they'd have to complete a term of compulsory service as commissioned officers. They didn't like the idea at all. It hung over them like a prison sentence. I listened with a sort of glazed look on my face as they spoke about this upcoming conscription.

When I returned home to Dublin, I forgot all about the two men who had so dazzled me for all of five days and my romantic imagination soon righted itself, especially as I knew I would never see them again. Or so I thought.

I soon got a job as a young freelance reporter for *Anois*, an Irish-language newspaper, and I spent the months of September and October skipping from one event to another, learning the job.

Then one day I waltzed back into the *Anois* offices in Merrion Square and the friendly sub-editor handed me a telephone number and told me I had missed a telephone call and that I was to contact the German submarine in the port. It was moored alongside a south-side quay, he said in Irish, a wide grin on his face.

I was confused, certain that something had been lost in translation. I berated myself at the paucity of my Irish vocabulary. A submarine! As I picked up the phone, the small newsroom crew smiled at my confusion and they waited to hear what would happen next. I listened to the dialling tone. When my call was picked up I heard the tell-tale sounds of disembodied voices and a whooshing sort of interference on the line. The penny dropped when I heard a voice relay my message over a tannoy and I remembered Heinrich and Christian just in time, seconds before one of them came on the line.

'Hello, this is Christian,' he said. He told me they were on the submarine with shore leave that evening and that they would love to meet me.

I felt my cheeks go red from a mixture of shyness and anxiety, and I experienced a terrible urge to run away, but I could not be so rude so I arranged to meet them on O'Connell Bridge at 6 p.m. I don't know why I suggested we meet on the central island of the bridge. In hindsight I think it was blind panic that made me suggest this very public spot. I suppose part of me worried that they might get lost or that I'd miss them.

I need not have worried. There they stood later that evening on the central island of O'Connell Street, the two tall Germans in full naval dress. Not a gold button or a white braided cord was missing. Every tassel and insignia imaginable was present on some part of their persons, from their peaked caps to their double-breasted jackets. They fairly took the wind out of my sails. I sidled up to them, knowing how inappropriate my Jesus sandals and casual clothes were. I felt the incongruity of our worlds keenly while they, in contrast, were only happy to see me. They hugged me, towering over me, still stark and stiff in their uniforms but desperately wanting to relax and feel the fresh Liffey air on their faces. And so we set off into the night.

I wish I'd been a more gracious host but I fairly raced them along until we were in off the street and settled in an anonymous bar in a nameless hotel where no one would see us. I kept watch the whole time in case someone who might know me happened along.

What was I afraid of? That someone would think these two exotic creatures, naval officers from a German submarine, were paying for my company; or that they were observing me, studying me like they would a creature in a zoo as part of some anthropological experiment.

And so I kept them out of sight. I did not consider their loneliness or their need for some lively companionship to divert them from the constricted lives they had on board the submarine. Even as we chatted I was completely taken up with planning how to be rid of them. After a few drinks I looked at my watch, as if I'd suddenly remembered something, and told them I had to go.

It was only 9 p.m. and not late at all when I stood on O'Connell Bridge to wave them off down the quays. As they walked off together, handsome, tall, their silhouettes in the glow of streetlights and the reflections from the river cast a spell on me and I felt the loss of their company and friendship. But I let them go and I knew for sure that night that I would never hear from or see them again.

45

Angela

The women outside my flat didn't intrude on my consciousness for a long while during the period when Miriam and I lived in a flat at the top of a tall Georgian building on Herbert Street in Dublin city centre. Miriam was nursing and I was working as a reporter for *The Sunday Tribune* at the time and the two of us had been there for a few months before I realised what was going on.

Snatches of their night-time conversations used to travel up, disembodied and removed – snatches of rows, of obscenities, of breaking glass, of songs, doors banging, brakes screeching, tyres crunching, a woman in heels running or stumbling. And I'd hear their swear words.

I'd hear them gathering down on the footpath on the wide doorstep outside our building. They were often right below my window, which was four stories up. They would sing 'The Fields of Athenry' or 'I Did It My Way'. I'd hear them cursing and, on occasion, I'd listen to them when they sang together in a drunken delirium, singing snatches of songs, great belters and songs of desire, like 'Delilah'. 'Why, why, why,' they'd sing, growing in volume as the chord reached its zenith. They'd sing out, emboldened and challenging, until a bottle smashed or a car pulled up and one of them had to hobble off, shoes clip-clopping on the concrete.

I used to have to smile at the self-awareness they seemed to imbue in those songs. They knew what they were doing. They knew where they were and what was happening in their lives. I used to wonder if I could help in some way but I wasn't sure how I could.

Sometimes it was only one woman who sat on the pavement and it was only when someone else joined her that I'd hear the timid beginnings of a song, songs by Rod Stewart or Dolly Parton. 'I Am Sailing' or 'Working Nine to Five'. 'Like a virgin, touched for the very first time.' The irony was never lost on them.

When they'd row, the venom and colour of their language shocked me – at first.

'Mary, Mary, come back. Come back and sing with me.'

'Fuck off, you cunt.'

And then their voices would disappear into the night.

Their slurred words never let me forget that they were drinking and all the time I'd hear the squeal of brakes. Heavy articulated lorries would pull up across the road and for a while the singing would be suspended. I knew too from the quiet when a woman was leaning in to a luxuriously upholstered car and then I'd listen to the smoothly running engine as it revved up to leave. It was clear what was happening.

During the day the street was light and airy. As I returned home in the late afternoon, I'd see couriers and taxis drive up at irregular intervals, going from one office to the next, and couples strolling hand in hand. At night, however, the place emptied and shadows flitting across the wide street and dark leafy trees would wave mysteriously from behind old-style Victorian railings.

I'd lie in bed listening, intrigued and slightly horrified by the goings-on outside, but like any voyeur I was attracted to the sounds and the stories they represented.

It was late one night when I came upon one of the women sitting alone on the steps of our building. She was leaning against the railings that led up to the front door. She was drinking from a naggin of vodka. It was close to midnight and bitterly cold. It was easy to see her in the streetlights as I came along. Her short skirt was hitched up unevenly around her hips. The curve of her buttocks was visible at the top of fleshy thighs under a pair of torn black tights. She sported a little ponytail at the back of her head. She made to move out of my way as I approached. She curled into herself and tried to stand up.

'Hello,' I said, addressing her. She seemed to turn in closer to the railings. 'Don't get up. You don't have to go,' I said. It was freezing but I was determined to reach out if I could. It was my chance. She muttered something.

'It's very cold tonight,' I said to her, nodding. I introduced myself. She looked at me warily for a moment and I think with a hint of shame, until suddenly her face cracked open and she smiled. Pointing to her chest, she said something. It was more of a rasping sound than a recognisable word. She repeated it again as if I was a half-wit. She said it patiently and with great slowness. Finally, I understood. It was her name.

'Oh, Angela!' I nodded. 'Would you like to come up for a cup of tea? I live just in here. You must be frozen out here.'

'No thanks, love. I'm all right. I have me bottle,' she said. And then in a rush: 'You know, once I have enough so me daughter can get married I'll be finished here.' She looked away towards the corner of the street. In a spill of words, she poured her story out. 'I have to make a bit of money … I've no choice, love. She got pregnant so I had to come out. The father is only fifteen and he's up before the courts in two months so he's got no money, he won't be able to pay for the wedding.'

A car pulled up further down the footpath and she moved off the step.

'I won't be doing this for much longer,' she said.

'If there's ever a night when you'd like a cup of tea, won't you ring my bell,' I told her.

'Right love, thanks,' she said, as she hurried towards the car.

I put the key in the door and pushed it in. When I had climbed up the stairs up to our flat, I looked down and watched her on the footpath. She'd moved off towards the car around the corner, flicking a cigarette butt away.

Although I often watched out for her, we soon moved to a different flat on a different street and though we were still on the south side of the city we were far away from any red light district, and so I never saw Angela again.

46

Gypsy King

It was Dublin in the 1990s and I had spread my wings as a journalist and started working freelance, writing feature articles and news stories for a range of publications including *The Irish Times*, *The Sunday Tribune*, the *Irish Examiner* and *The Dubliner*, as well as working occasionally in broadcasting doing reviews and reports for the Irish-language radio station, Raidió na Gaeltachta.

As I began to get more and more work in the newsroom of *The Irish Times*, I came to love the life. My uncle, Donal Foley, had been news editor and deputy editor of the paper over many years. He'd died in 1981 but he was still spoken of with great affection in the newsroom. His son, Michael, and his daughter, Deirdre, were working there when I was in the newsroom, so the Foley family was well represented, and it felt good to be part of it.

Each day I'd go in and wait to be assigned a news story.

'Catherine,' an editor might say, passing a scrap of paper to me with a couple of typed lines and a phone number. 'Ring around and see what you can get on this.'

The editors who sat at a central desk in the newsroom occupied the seats of power. They decided what stories were important and to whom they'd assign them. When they looked across at the reporters' rows of desks, which were positioned at right angles to their console, they'd wait to catch some reporter's eye and ask them to follow up on the day's breaking story. We called the particular row of desks which was directly in front of the editors 'Snipers' Alley'.

Our ears pricked to hear the radio's signature tune for the 1 p.m. news, which signified that the morning was over and the day had kicked into life. As it got later, the pace quickened again and editors started reassigning stories or began marching over to discover how you were progressing. When the evening deadline loomed, more reporters would come rushing back to write up their stories. The noise levels would rise then, more fluorescent lights would come on and editors would again come looking for stories, shouting and harrying us.

And so on Friday and Saturday nights, after a week of working in highly-pressurised newsrooms, press photographers, reporters, sub-editors, sports-writers, freelancers and other city centre folk would go out to unwind and meet fellow hacks.

That's how I came to meet him first.

He was wearing a scuffed leather jacket and a khaki shirt. He sported a tan. As he sashayed across to us, there was an air of exoticism about him. Someone whispered that he'd recently returned from Shanghai. A trilby hung nonchalantly from one of his hands.

The bevelled newels, mantel mirrors, red velvet banquettes and mahogany counters of the Victorian bar suited him well. His dark hair fell down over his forehead and wafted back along a frayed collar. As he came towards us, he seemed to swamp all in his path with bonhomie, moving with the grace of a ballet dancer, throwing his arms out with arabesque-like flamboyance to greet friends. He pushed through the press of bodies and emerged in front of me as if newly sprung from a raging sea.

'Hello,' he said, smiling wickedly. He looked at me as if we shared a secret and I nodded, throwing off the ennui I'd been feeling. I was immediately captivated and speechless. But I soon found my voice and we began to chat. He was a charming rogue, who exuded fun and warmth. There was a definite sparkle in his eye.

'I've seen your by-line,' he said, soft-soaping my ego. 'Was that your story the other day on the front page?'

I was immediately smitten. When he was leaving he entreated me to come with him and I did. As we stepped out of the bar, he dropped the trilby onto my head.

We walked into the night together, up along Grafton Street, then passing the Shelbourne Hotel and Doheny & Nesbitt. Wandering down Baggot Street, the literary ghosts of people who hover over that stretch of Dublin seemed to wag their fingers at us.

When he leaned over to kiss me in the criss-cross shadow of the trees I felt a frisson of excitement. It seemed as if we were swaying in the breeze while his eyes twinkled under the brim of his hat. The kiss was brief but it left me reeling and when he turned to go at the junction of Fitzwilliam Street, I watched him go off towards Merrion Row, like Top Cat or Don Juan, insouciant and devil-may-care.

Some weeks later he cooked me dinner in his flat. I simpered innocently when I discovered that he was living over a brothel and that he seemed to know each of the women by name. It was so typical of him to be curious, charming and impartial. He was never judgemental. As he mentioned his downstairs neighbours, with true Casanova diffidence, he gave me ice cream with rum, banana and chocolate dressing for dessert.

Gypsy King

We went to parties together and we often stayed out late. I remained at his side, waiting for a further demonstration of affection, looking up at him before we'd go our separate ways, my lips parted coquettishly in hopeful expectation. Usually he'd lean over and wrap me in a great bear hug.

He was my version of Mr Darcy and Mr Rochester rolled into one. He was a colossus who strode through the city late into the night, striding up dark streets to the next party, the next concert. Often when he returned after a trip abroad, he'd bring me presents – little bangles and scarves, coloured woven purses and the like. And still, I hoped that our next kiss would happen and become the beginning of something between us.

One night in a nightclub we listened to the Gypsy Kings and, my heart in my mouth, I asked him if he wouldn't like to become more serious, to make a commitment. As the music boomed out, he nursed his drink.

'Ah, now, don't you know you're like a sister to me,' he said, covering a sort of embarrassment. Clubbers around us heaved as one on the little dance floor, swirling and swinging in time to the salsa beat. Soon he moved away to make eyes at a dark-haired beauty.

He fulfilled all the criteria of what I was looking for in a boyfriend – tall, handsome, charming, roguish, funny and elusive – and so I couldn't stop hoping. Until one night after he'd fallen asleep on his couch, the debris of his travels scattered around the room, I sat beside him, waiting, the empty grate staring blankly at me like a warning. Quietly the idea of romance seemed to evaporate. So I let myself out and flagged a taxi, shaking my head at the idiocy of it all.

It was months before I saw him again, walking up Grafton

Street. I stepped quickly into a doorway and watched him, feeling the cold dispassion and displacement of a spy. His coat swung open, his hair and profile stark against the cityscape in the afternoon sun. I imagined him years into the future still going to parties, still weaving his spell and all that remained that day was a widening of the gap between us.

When he'd gone, I carried on. Passing by Molly Malone and her cart, I had to pull my coat tight against the cold and I told myself to remain stoic as I faced into the chugging buses and biting breeze along Westmoreland Street.

47

My Street

There were three young rowan trees across the street from my house in the Liberties in Dublin. My mother said these trees were lucky. They bore red berries in the spring and their frayed leaves were like yellow hands, bony and long-fingered.

After a number of years in rented accommodation, I moved into my new house in the Liberties in the spring of 2001, even while the house was still being damp-proofed, dry-lined, rewired and painted. I was now a grown-up with a permanent and pensionable job as a journalist with *The Irish Times*. I even had a mortgage.

In the summer the leaves of the rowans turned a darker green. Sometimes I saw little boys running under the branches but that didn't happen too often, because the trees were off-limits, really, in a narrow space behind the tall railings that front a block of flats.

This was a nicely proportioned four-storey block that was art deco in design, as a knowledgeable architect friend once told me. I swelled with pride the day he told me. We both looked across at my new inner city neighbours, and enjoyed the straight lines that curved stylishly at the top around windows and corners, the ridged divisions between the storeys and the newly cleaned, red-sandstone brickwork.

On another day, my next-door neighbour told me that my street ran along good lay lines, which are ancient, straight 'paths' or routes in the landscape that are believed to have spiritual significance. I knew immediately that she was right. All the signs for a fair sailing in my new home were good.

The street was in the city centre, located near a busy junction where the cars whizzed by. Some of my neighbours had lived here all their lives. Occasionally they sat on their front steps and took the sun, hidden behind the parked cars. Sometimes they stood chatting in their doorways and watched the world go by as the evening came in.

At night I heard the couples and groups of friends going home from the pub – singing, shouting, cursing, roaring, contradicting each other – and I smiled at the stories that were unfolding underneath my window. I imagined I was living in Pigale, the red-light district of Paris, when there were fierce fights below and I sometimes wondered if I would find a body lying in a pool of blood on the footpath the next day. But the voices usually faded and they passed along up the street, making their way home. Their anger died out gradually and as it got later and quieter all I heard were the cars swishing by and, once the Luas had been built, I'd hear the driver ringing the bell as he motored towards the stop at St James's Hospital. It used to sound like a special goodnight salute to me and to all of us in our beds listening to the night – *ding, ding*, he seemed to say. *Ding, ding!*

I often thought of the family that grew up in my house before I lived there. When I first got the key I walked through the rooms gingerly in case I disturbed anyone – even though I knew it was empty. Still, I jumped when I saw an old walking stick and a forgotten green plastic Christmas tree lying in the corner of an old wardrobe upstairs. For a moment, it was as if I had intruded on someone else's time and space.

My Street

Voices echo through a house, words reverberate on a stairway, on a landing, sounds of pots and pans in a kitchen must surely leave an imprint. I wonder is there a way of recapturing those incidental noises – of children talking, of parents whispering, of visitors laughing – and replaying them. Do sounds of a family remain in the space to be discovered, to be replayed? Sometimes in the evening when I came in, I found myself saying hello to the empty hallway – half in response to a feeling that the house had been waiting in silence for me to return and half in response to the sounds that had once filled its rooms.

I think that's why I love Walter de la Mare's poem, 'The Listeners':

> 'Is there anybody there?' said the Traveller
> Knocking on the moonlit door; …
> And he smote upon the door again a second time;
> 'Is there anybody there?' he said.
> But no one descended to the Traveller.

Of course, I'd have jumped out of my skin if anyone had 'descended to me' in my house. Thankfully it was the same for me as it was for the traveller:

> No head from the leaf-fringed sill
> Leaned over and looked into his grey eyes,
> Where he stood perplexed and still.

However, as in the poem, there was a sense in my new place that there was another level of sound, another level of presence, that there was a host of phantom listeners that dwelt in the lone

house then, who were witness to me as they had been to the
traveller:

> Ay, they heard his foot upon the stirrup,
> And the sound of iron on stone.

When I first moved in I set about stripping the walls. There
were several layers of wallpaper in each room – I peeled each
strip away and I got a glimpse of the other eras, like the times
when yellow roses were the ultimate in chic or a lilac flock motif
was chosen by the woman of the house for the master bedroom.
There was a pink horizontal print too, and brown and orange
circles that I'm sure must have dated from the 1970s. It seemed
as if a family's history was there, waiting to be understood. There
were light fittings and finishes that were evidence of forgotten
styles from the 1960s and even earlier.

I knew that the elderly man who had lived in the house
before I moved in had reared his family here. I imagined him
and his wife as they were when they'd moved in first as a young
couple. It must have been back in the 1940s.

After stripping another layer in the small bedroom, I discovered that they, the previous owners, had at some point decided
to paper and decorate the room in a deep mauve colour. I wondered what year they'd decided to do this and at what point in
their lives they'd been. They must have chosen the paper and
matched it with a certain colour of paint, with light fittings and
a style of carpet or linoleum for the floor. I hoped they were
happy and I'm sure they were – one or two of the neighbours
mentioned them to me, and I also felt they were happy because
the house in its stillness possessed a pleasant calm.

My Street

Yes, the more I thought about it, I came to believe that a family's memories could linger in a space, that their voices only need to be tuned into in order to be heard. I wondered if I would leave my memories behind too, to settle in corners, to resonate from the bricks.

Time slipped away, of course, and I am no longer living in that house. When it's empty again will the silence surge softly backwards, as de la Mare puts it? Even if I'd like to leave an imprint – a sense of my time in that house, a sense perhaps that I was in tune with the vibrations – I suppose, in the end, all you will hear is the silence.

48

In Mick O'Dea's Studio

Mick O'Dea is an award-winning artist who has had many exhibitions and commissions over the years. He is a member of Aosdána and president of the Royal Hibernian Academy. In 2004 he was continuing his fascination with people, their faces and the stories they have to tell, by working towards an exhibition of forty-four portraits that would be shown in the Kevin Kavanagh Gallery. They were to be a collection of people who worked and lived in and around the city centre. As a journalist I was one of the people who was asked if I'd consider sitting for my portrait.

The studio was located on the fourth floor of a house at the top of a cobbled street, at a spot where the traffic noises dropped away as soon as you turned into it to go up towards those tall tawny-coloured houses that date back to the 1730s. There's a hush there and you can listen for echoes of children at play or carts rolling over the cobblestones from days gone by.

I climbed flights of shallow stairs up to his studio, a high-ceilinged, bright room that looked like a set from a Sean O'Casey play. An old mantelpiece, an ancient fireplace with a blackened hearth and chimney breast, an uneven floor and a number of cracks in the glass of the windows all added to an atmosphere that was from another time. If there was a clock, it would surely have been a grandfather clock and its hands would be stuck at half past eight or one o'clock, never to move again. There was a feeling that time in this large, cold room was being distilled, or even slowed down. O'Dea had canvasses, pots of paint, easels, brushes, jars, rags, pencils, chalk, wooden pallets, pieces of wood and finished paintings sitting, perched or standing up against every shelf, surface and table.

This was my first experience of sitting for my portrait. I was apprehensive and curious. O'Dea told me to make myself comfortable on the sturdy leather-bound chair that was positioned on a raised platform. I sat into it, chose one spot on the window to stare at and stayed still for just over three hours. I was able to stretch whenever I needed to. I could look at him or far into the distance. I chose to look out through the window.

O'Dea painted energetically; using his brush like a sextant or a spyglass, he held it out from him and squinted as he gauged distances. The smell of oil and turpentine grew stronger as the morning wore on. What did he see, I wondered. Could he read my thoughts? What would I do if I got a cramp? I thought about time passing, about death and destiny and faith and fate as I watched the clouds move slowly across the grey sky outside. There wasn't a hint of blue there that day. All I heard were the soft sounds of deft brush strokes scratching across the canvas.

I continued to look out the north-facing window. It was a cold, dull day, glassed in by an opaque sky. An odd seagull flew across the sky. A steady light filled the room. I liked sitting there and I enjoyed the whole experience. It was precious time. It gave me an opportunity to reflect and savour the day.

There was a table on a plinth behind a screen. There were other occasional pieces of furniture in the room, such as an old chaise longue. We had our lunch sitting on this, studying the portraits that were already hanging around the room.

I wasn't allowed look at the painting until the end. When we broke for lunch, I stretched and climbed off the platform to look around at some of the paintings stacked up against the walls. There were paintings of other individuals. I wondered what kind of people they were. Who was the girl with the cup in her hand looking off into the distance in such a relaxed, almost indifferent way? Is she like that? How could she be so nonchalant when involved in such a creative process, I wondered. She's another artist, O'Dea said. What about the intense young man who looked right out at me with piercing eyes? Is he like that in person? And the tall, handsome man who stands looking at me with complete calm, as if he was ready to take on any challenge. Or the elderly man who had wise, calm eyes.

O'Dea had painted each of them sympathetically. He spoke openly about his experiences with people who had sat for their portraits in the past. In the case of one man, it seemed to threaten him, he said. It was as if he felt the way some primitive people feel when they believe a photographer is trying to rob them of their soul.

When I first saw my own portrait I was confused. It seemed to rush at me; it seemed a mess of startling and slithering paint that was still wet and viscous. After my eyes adjusted, I continued to look at it, to take it in. I wanted to view it from every distance and angle. I felt a bit unmasked, and yet I couldn't get enough of it. *So this is the way I look*, I thought. I was shocked and pleased at the same time. I was sorry I couldn't stay looking at it for the rest of the day, a bit like Narcissus.

Before I left, I looked back at all of the portraits ranged around the studio. Three deep on some walls, others stacked against windows and chairs, it struck me that the paintings formed a kind of chorus, mute yet deafening in the energy they emitted. It was an orchestra of feeling that had been captured in oil. The clothes and the haircuts placed us in 2004 but the expressions and the concerns were ageless. The eyes, the postures, the hands, the tilt of the heads, the mouths, the looks, the hairlines, the laugh lines – there was a great warmth in all of them. They could have been from any time, any century. What a tragedy to split them up, I thought. Each portrait was separate and yet connected to the next by our shared experience of sitting for the artist. Grouped like this, they seemed to represent a gathering of humanity – a collective that belonged together.

I have the painting in my possession still. My face is riven with an intensity that pleases me. I am glad to know that I looked like that. It reminds me of the road that I was travelling.

49

Frawley's

Frawley's department store on Thomas Street in the Liberties is gone now. The shop had been a presence on the street for over 100 years, but it closed its doors forever in 2007. In its final years, when I used to wander in, it had begun to wind down and had become a sleepy place of business. It was the place I loved most to go shopping.

From the first day I wandered in there, I found it restful and easy in its unpretentious dowdiness. I loved the value to be had in its range of sheets and pillowcases. I waded past its hip-high counters in a soft glow of relaxation. It became a sort of retreat and sanctuary for me. I'd meander in there on days when I needed to escape 'this workaday world' and I'd relax, looking through plastic bathroom accessories and shelves of out-of-season Christmas decorations. It felt like a home-from-home.

It harked back to another time. It felt like a church in some ways but it was also non-judgemental. There was no sense that God and the saints and the souls might be watching. I didn't have to imagine them frowning or shaking a finger at me in disapproval. Frawley's made no demands. I'd spend an hour happily rummaging through shelves of cotton quilt covers, voluminous and minuscule towels, and extravagantly coloured shower curtains. Whether I spent money or not seemed to be a matter of indifference to the staff. The motley collection of shoppers who rambled in did not excite the assistants too greatly and that is a balm to any browser. The assistants usually chatted amongst themselves, engrossed in their conversations, laughing, but ready to be helpful if necessary. They allowed us shoppers to take our time and go to a till at our leisure. They'd serve in a most languorous and elegant fashion. It made me feel happy and blessed.

I bought extra large pale blue and pink bloomers from the hosiery department for my petite mother at home to make her laugh and to keep her warm. She heard the ad for *Frawley's for All of Yous* on the radio one day and recognised it as the place I raved about. I told her how I roamed the aisles of the shop in search of bargains and she used to imagine me there.

They stocked highly useful items, such as the full range of hoover bags, all manner of fuses, cheap but essential moisturising creams and lotions, as well as shampoo and hair conditioner for hair of every hue and texture. I bought a green dressing gown there once. I bought a pair of jeans for twenty euros – the kind that artists wear when they work in oils on large canvasses – and these were admired by one and all. I bought sheets to beat the band, duvet covers to fit a landlady's double bed and a brass coal scuttle with its own matching shovel that still shines brilliantly by the fire on a winter's night. There was a jumble of jazz and soul CDs on offer upstairs, plus old-fashioned and up-to-the-minute DVDs. I used to dangle my fingers over the titles, feeling decadent at the wanton waste of my time on such frivolities and carrying on regardless.

I got trousers for my father, which had a tailor's special pleat in the waistband at the back in order to allow the fold to expand when seated, as the draper's assistant pointed out to me. I was gently assisted and directed in all my choices. I bought bulbs, old-fashioned oilcloths for my kitchen table and sieves, colanders and chopping boards for next to nothing.

Maybe I was drawn in there because the floors of worn linoleum reminded me of my grandmother's kitchen long ago. They had that lovely solid, yet softly sinking feeling underfoot. It was so familiar to walk on. Or was it that my fellow customers were busy looking for bargains and trying to make ends meet, not wanting to strike a pose or strut a certain noughties' style? This was a zone of wearisome commerce. It was like stepping into a lukewarm bath.

I often hesitated at the door, when that feeling of familiarity was too cloying to be endured. Would I go in or not? Some days I would not go in at all, gagging on the shop's requirement to submit to its weary, old-fashioned vibe. Most days, however, it was just what I needed. The ambience, the tone and tenor of the shop lapped about me and enveloped me in its calm, gravy-like easiness.

As a new house owner, I picked up many a useful knick-knack. To me, the shop was a jewel in the Liberties. It was my Mecca on days when life was sharply etched in shrieks and frenzy. Frawley's, familiar and undemanding, called out to me, a stopping-off place where I could take a breath and think, wonder about my life and where I was headed, wonder if God in the church across the street was missing me, watching me or even aware of me.

I loved earwigging in Frawley's, feeling like a modern-day Proust. The staff often carried on complicated conversations, such as about the rights and wrongs of a relationship. As they batted back and forth – while serving a customer and packing a bag – the balance of power between the two assistants could tip dangerously from benign and friendly to suspicious and intolerant. I still recall the face of a determined young cashier with nervous eyes and pouting mouth, authoritatively staring down her young underling. In comparison, the underling's pliant nature with bristling skin reminded me of the pointillism I had once seen in an exhibition on impressionism in the Tate.

The shop is gone now and I wander the streets looking for a new sanctum. I sometimes go through the doors of the darkened church across the road from where Frawley's used to be and settle there for a moment to think. It's not the same; I never come away with a bargain.

I will always be grateful and nostalgic for Frawley's. It was a faithful friend of sorts, giving me my first foothold in the Liberties when I moved there. One could never forget a friend like that, and more so if they are no longer with us.

50

Crogal

I own a painting of a black bird, a fierce, prehistoric kind of creature who stands tall in the centre of the canvas. He has the stony, watchful eye of a carrion crow that has been interrupted in the act of devouring something vital. It's a big painting and he takes up the whole of the canvas. It's a view of him from the side. He's got the ungainly body of a big, lumbering bird of prey.

Hanging on the wall over my fireplace in the Liberties, his blackness compliments the sooty grate of the fireplace underneath. There's a link there that I don't quite understand but the mirrored blackness is mesmerising.

I'm not sure if my bird is a crow or an eagle. It's hard to say, but I'm nearly sure he's male because he has a look about him that hints at defiance and maleness. There's a striking immutability about him. The one pin-eye that is trained on me, guarded and wary, has me in his field of vision.

I'm sure he's graceful and terrifying in flight but he's captured on the ground here. He's nervous because he was clearly in the process of eating some class of an egg. He looks as if he has possibly heard something and, holding his position, he has raised his head to scan for predators. His food is like the yolk of an egg that has spilled out of the shell in one great glob of yellow and mustard.

It's a painting by the artist Mick Mulcahy from west Waterford, a painter of great power. He was a young man when he painted this beast of a bird in the late 1970s. He had yet to travel to places like the Sahara, the outback of Australia, to Papua New Guinea and to Korea, where he would portray indigenous peoples and their natural environments – an endeavour for which he was to become well known. Back then he was staying with his father in Helvick and my aunts, Sheila and Gile, were near neighbours.

He presented the painting to them as a gift one day, carrying it in to them under his arm, offering it to them the way he does, pleased, confident and proud of his work. They may have had a drink to celebrate or my Auntie Gile may have prompted a little round of applause. I know they were all in agreement that it was powerful. It was a creature that was somewhere between a crow, an eagle and a black gull. Together the three of them came up with a name and christened it that day when he stood it on a chair and they stood back to look at it. CROGAL, they said. And Mick wrote that in pencil on the side of the frame.

The painting hung for years in their dining room. I always loved its colour and its strangeness. Years later, when Auntie Gile died, the painting was left to me in her will.

Crogal's backdrop is a swirling whorl of colour. It circles him, rotating around him in a heady mix of geometric and circular designs in warm reds, ochres and yellow tints. There are zigzag sections and red markings, the likes of which you might see on a totem pole.

His beak is long and curved and red like the caked mud of an equatorial riverbed. He's got nobility and a vulnerability about him, even if he's fierce and watchful.

He watches me now, Crogal. I don't think he's nervous any more. He appears calmer to me now, somehow. His rich yolky egg has remained untouched since it was painted, so he's happy to stand and remind me of his story – of his creation in Helvick Head by Mulcahy when seagulls were squawking and squealing outside the windows, demanding to be flung onto his canvasses instead of this black interloper from another time, when savage hunger and satiation were the only laws and life was a jungle full of colour and verdant tangles. Crogal is happy to remind me of his growth as an heirloom and of his journey to my house in Dublin.

As a teenager, I would stand and admire Crogal when I visited my aunts. I loved the brazenness of the bird's blue-black plumage. I loved the strangeness of it. It was a great furnace of colour, vibrating in the corner of their cream-coloured dining room. Over the years cigarette smoke filled the room as they talked and reminisced and the walls faded slowly to a coffee-coloured beige. But Crogal's colours never faded. Today he is as steady and black and vibrant as ever, standing guard.

51

Dusty Books

I love owning old books and papers, especially those that once belonged to relatives I never knew. They can contain all manner of information about another time. They can shed light into someone else's mind and provide a glimpse of life as it was in a distant past.

I took great care of where I shelved them when I moved into my new house in the Liberties. I raided our shelves at home and brought a number of them back to Dublin with me. I liked having them around me. I always grouped the old ones together – it seemed like a natural fit.

Sometimes, it is the books that are missing pages and covers, eaten by mites and falling apart at the seams that mean more to me than newer, shinier ones. I particularly love old schoolbooks, especially the ones that are signed with a youthful scrawl and possibly dated. It's fascinating to leaf through *Enquire Within Upon Everything*, for example. This is a great compendium of information from the Victorian age. It was first published in 1856. There's no signature on this book, but it was purchased in Mitchell's Book Store at Cangallo in Buenos Aires, so I presume it was bought in the early 1920s by William Ryan of Waterford, a cousin on my mother's side whose father was a sea captain but who himself worked for many years with the railways in South America, and who, according to family lore, knew Eva Perón.

I believe he was quite a serious, distant man. He married

but he was not particularly loving or kind. Maybe he was a bit like this book: full of quaint, erudite details and facts, if perhaps short on emotion and humour. According to the publisher's preface to this, the one-hundred-and-thirteenth edition, proof of the book's worldwide popularity is clearly shown by the record number of copies sold. Sales reached the wonderful total of 1,500,000 copies, a number which the publishers, Herbert Jenkins Limited of London, believed in 1923 to be 'absolutely without precedent'.

And when one 'enquires within', there are all manner of tables and titbits, tips and antiquated information. There are suggestions on proper conduct and manners, sections on dinner parties, balls and evening parties. A gentleman's calling card, for example, should measure 3 x 1.5 inches, while a lady's should be 3.5 x 2.5 inches. The surface should be slightly glazed; the edges must not be gilt.

There are gardening hints, medical information, food and cookery, legal information, general information, household hints and miscellaneous receipts. I like to think that William Ryan used this book a great deal. It would have appealed to his mathematical, engineering side. There's a section on poisons, on the care of infants, on how to wash a white lace veil and so on.

Another book that I value is an old tattered copy of a catechism, entitled *A Companion to the Catechism: Designed Chiefly for the Use of Young Catechists and Heads of Families*. This belonged to my paternal grandfather, who signed it on 2 September 1903 in a strong, clear hand – Daniel Joseph Foley. He was seventeen at the time. He was born in 1886.

It must have been the start of the academic year at the De La Salle School in Waterford. His brother Pat signed it five years later on the same date, 2 September 1908, so they must have shared it. It's an old hardback and it was bought in P. M. Egan's shop, bookseller and stationer, of 78, the Quay, Waterford, as a stamp on an inside page testifies. It was published in 1897 by M. H. Gill & Son of 50 Upper O'Connell Street, Dublin.

There's an old piece of blue blotting paper, frail and thin, lying between two of the pages with the lines of a religious poem written by Dan entitled 'Jesus Sold' on it. Here's the last verse:

> Erring men,
> Love again,
> Give sinning o'er,
> War no more,
> But follow him.

It's the simple sincerity of his young heart that is so appealing to me. Underneath this, he appears to ask the future co-owner of the book, his brother Pat, what he thinks of the poem. *Cad é do mheas air, a Phádraig*, he writes. Pat must have given a verbal response as there's no written trace of what he thought.

The book's question and answer format is accessible even though it deals with complex theoretical abstracts. In one chapter the student is asked if servants are obliged to protect their masters from wrong. How should masters treat their servants, it asks on the next page. It is clear the book is from another era when Heaven and Hell, sin and sacrifice, masters and servants were daily realities; where concepts such as absolution, remarkable visions and fast days were accepted readily and without question.

Dan Foley's teenage signature is full of conviction and

confidence. The official stamp of the Boys' School, Ferrybank, Waterford is here too, proof that Dan – who was headmaster there until he died at the age of fifty in the summer of 1937 – must have used this catechism right through his life. He's also written a few notes in pencil on a page at the back, possibly in the run-up to an examination, which is another word he's written in pencil on this same page. These notes include the words 'subjection, pain, grief, darkness of understanding, weakness of will, inclination to evil'.

What a book! What a schooling young people had then.

Oh to have known these men who read and loved books, to have looked into their eyes and asked them questions about life and love, age and time. I turn the pages of their books carefully, lovingly even, waiting to unearth another particle of information that will give me a further glimpse into what they and their lives may have been like. Sometimes it is the absence of a mark that can prove beguiling and mystifying. But a mark in the margin, a dog-eared or torn page or a written word can reveal so much that it leaves me puzzling over it for a long time and I let my imagination run riot.

52

Guatemala

The minibus drove us as high up the mountain as it could go. Then we walked. The path wound steeply up through tall trees. Through the branches we could see other mountains rearing up into the sky, ranged around us at every point. It was hot; from the air, you might have seen vivid slashes of bright green and orange earth.

We climbed up to a small Mayan village on a level with the highest peaks. I was in Guatemala with a group of journalists who had been invited by Trócaire, the Irish charity and overseas development agency, to visit some of the places where its volunteers were working so that we could report on its campaign to seek justice for the country's indigenous Maya people.

It was quiet in the tiny, grieving Guatemalan village of Xecotz. The ground was covered with soft clay so all movement was hushed. The bare feet of children and their parents walking along earthen lanes left only the smallest imprint. We saw the earth squish beneath them. We followed in our sturdy boots. All sounds were dulled as we made our way to their little church. A cock yodelled on a post, alerting us all to the coming of night.

And then the darkness fell quickly, blanketing us until we had to grope our way along a path. Still, looking up high above us, we could see that the sky was clear and the stars were twinkling in an inky universe.

We went into the roughly built chapel where many of the

local people had already gathered. Great big eyes watched us from the pews when we sat on the benches on the right-hand side of the chapel. There were whispers in the dim light. Little boys, some with swollen bellies, stood nearby and pressed in close to their mothers. Three men strummed on guitars in a corner, their music thin and scratchy. They seemed out of tune, jangling and weak with no melody and no strength behind their hymns.

Mayan families were in the process of saying goodbye – a ceremony that was due to finish before the sun came up – to the family members who'd disappeared during the civil war. The bodies had only recently been discovered, exhumed from a mass grave. Now, they were to be given a proper burial at dawn and we'd been invited by Trócaire to witness the ceremony on the understanding that we would write about it, thereby drawing attention to it in the wider world and also highlighting the plight of these people, who had endured terrible brutality and injustice throughout a war of genocide perpetrated against them from 1960 to 1996.

When we were there in the mid-2000s the Maya people were in the process of bringing the perpetrators of that genocide to court and Trócaire was helping them to achieve this. Many horrific things occurred during the genocide in Guatemala; for example, during 1981 and 1982 the army and paramilitary groups murdered 100,000 people.

As we travelled through the country and interviewed various individuals, I sometimes felt that we were intruding on their grief. I worried that we had no right to quiz these people, who were there to answer our questions about their experiences of having lost their families, or being raped or beaten. They told us that they wanted us to witness and report on their suffering. Ever since, I remember how they looked at us and explained that it was important that we were there.

And so we all huddled close on the benches as the vigil continued, us westerners trying to understand what they'd been through. It was a night to think about their souls, it was an *oíche na marbh* (a night of the dead) to remember forever.

The church felt like an old-fashioned school classroom. All the coffins were piled high in rows, one on top of another. They were light-coloured, small, newly made, still rough and sticky from the sap seeping from the light wooden structures.

The shaman – a thin man in narrow white pants and a dark purple coat – swung a thurible and the sweet smell of incense filled the space as the sad, empty night wore on. Before the sun came up, the men stopped playing their instruments and joined others to carry the coffins outside. They went down the side of the mountain towards a long, communal grave they'd dug, where they would bury the bodies of thirty-three loved ones from their community.

We followed the procession of mourners – toddlers, old people and young boys. There were solemn faces; they seemed weary, too spent to cry. As they gathered along the top of the trench, we saw the dawn breaking and the sun's first rays begin to peep over the distant horizon.

As the ceremony began, the dark nearby peaks began to change, turning a pinky orange, blushing. The dim light spread. Now, it began to change to yellow and the light lit up the trench. The ochre clay was piled in heaps and the gash in the earth was red and glistening, open like a wound.

The shaman stood on a rise and swung the thurible again and

again as the sun rose. The musicians started another scratchy hymn, strumming loose strings, their grey trilby hats looked as worn as their eyes. More men, all thin and small-boned – their wide-brimmed hats stark against the red clay – got into the trench and started taking the coffins from those on top, trying not to jolt them. No one spoke as the boxes were passed from one to the other. Some boxes fell awkwardly. Once all the coffins had been placed in the trench, the men climbed out and began shovelling in the red clay. It was nearly over.

The shaman, standing on a pile of red earth, chanted softly. It sounded like he was saying a decade of the rosary. The incense from his thurible wafted back and forth, a smudge of lilac against a white sky. We hung our heads low, trying to imagine what terrible events had happened in Guatemala, to leave them so *cloíte mar seo*, so defeated like this, so broken.

53

The Berber Women

The Berber guide and I were sitting on the floor, our backs against a whitewashed wall. We were studying the carpets that had been unfurled at our feet. Their geometric designs were hypnotic. I stared at all the repeated abstract shapes – the lines and lines of little crosses that were woven into the rugs. They had a mysterious pull. The Berber tribeswomen at the other end of the room sat on the floor, watching, possibly hoping I was going to buy something, while the guide spoke, directing my attention back to a particular carpet in front of me with a tiny star at the core of its design.

'See the four points of the cross and the point at its heart,' he said. 'These are the five points of a star. They correspond to the five elements of wisdom.' He listed these five elements on his fingers: silence, emptiness, wideness, purity and the light of stars.

I looked down at the dark-skinned women who had woven the rugs, lacing designs into a pattern to represent the wisdom of their ancestry. They watched me with sparkling eyes, waiting, their burkas tucked in around them. But I was no bargain hunter and in the end I didn't buy any rug.

Back in the daylight, the air was filled with the sounds of Arabic traders selling their wares. I walked through the outdoor market, known as a *souk*. Its narrow passageways wound through rows of ancient stalls, home to a variety of different trades. There was a cobbler sitting at a counter mending shoes; in another booth a man was sharpening knives using a kind of bicycle to power his lathe. I passed a stall where stacks of spices were piled high on a display wagon and in another little booth a barefoot man covered in navy dye was stepping into a vat of black liquid to stamp on a sheep's fleece. Around the next corner, I walked into a swarm of flies buzzing around the head of a camel, held aloft on a spike over a butcher's counter.

I felt like Princess Leah in *Star Wars*, wandering through her galaxy, so when the snake charmer beckoned me across, hoisting a great snake up out of a basket at his feet and draping it around his neck, I didn't start away. The man handled the snake firmly, stroking it. He coaxed me over, nodding and beckoning. I went closer, keeping my eye on the python. The lugubrious serpent hardly moved. The noise and the frenzy of the place filled me with resolve. I nodded and in a second it was around me, its weight tight around my neck and across my back. It was cool like leather, heavy, and I didn't mind at all.

Later that day, RoseAnn and I travelled in the heat of the lower slopes of the High Atlas Mountains in Morocco. We were in a minibus, driving past tall medieval castle walls and turrets, sand-coloured locations where *Lawrence of Arabia* was shot in 1962 and then in 1999 where they filmed *Gladiator*. And now, a few short years after that film was made, RoseAnn and I – along with a small group of trekkers – were in the very same area, heading for a little village in the mountains.

Going along bumpy, potholed roads, we passed olive groves, grazing camels and young shepherds resting under palm trees out of the heat, their flocks nearby. When the driver turned up a narrow lane shaded by trees and rocks, the air grew cooler.

The Berber Women

Once we'd disembarked, we carried on by foot, bringing all our belongings with us, walking for the rest of the day along a stony track. It curved by the side of a dry riverbed. We went higher all the time, often stepping over treacherous dips. We had to watch our step along that path and not be distracted by the changing landscape that went from barren, rocky gorges to lush, green stretches. When I looked down I could see the dried bed of the river below, strewn with boulders, as if they'd been sprinkled over the caked mud by a mighty celestial hand.

We were hungry as we trudged along. Towards evening we had our eyes peeled for a sight of the village. Then we heard a sharp, clear noise like a bark. I listened out for another sound but there was nothing. We carried on until I was sure I heard a donkey braying. I turned and so did the others but there was no animal in sight.

We walked ever upwards until we saw the village, sitting on the edge of the mountain just ahead of us, cut off from the world. I heard the laugh of a goat and I searched the rocks for a sign of it.

As we neared the houses, we began to hear the sound of more farmyard animals. We heard chickens clucking and ducks quacking. I scanned the rocks but there was no sign of any animals. Before we reached the little lanes that ran between the huts, we were all bemused at the chorus of animal noises that were trumpeting our arrival – quacking, clucking, crowing and braying, all chiming one after the other – and I smiled as they began to reveal themselves – the mischievous boys in the evening shadows.

They were perched on the tallest rocks, cheeky smirks and darting bright eyes in the deepening light, all peering at us, all delighted we'd been duped. As we passed near their lookouts, they carried on mimicking the sounds of domestic animals. We had to laugh. Their croaks and cries were so realistic, each sound a perfect imitation.

They were too shy to come any closer. I could just make out their white teeth gleaming in the twilight. By the time we arrived, they had vanished. This isolated village, so cut off from the world, reminded me of the Great Blasket.

Our guide led us to the house where we were to stay for the night. He prepared a meal for us. After eating, I stepped out to admire the night sky. There in the dimness, like a ghost, was the mountain, its great brooding immensity blocking most of my view. If it shifted the village would be lost. As I stood there I was filled with a sense of its power. In its height, its proximity, it was a mass like no other. Its immensity hinted at an even mightier, more mysterious power.

I went inside, shivering from the night air, nervous and alert, dwelling on the glimpse I'd got into the gaping mouth of the heavens. We were to leave early the next day and trek along the upper slopes of the mountain range. As I lay down on my sleeping bag, it was only the braying of a donkey and the bark of a dog in the darkness that comforted me and made me smile.

⤛ ⤜

When we were only halfway through our trek in Morocco, we had already accumulated so much luggage that we decided to send clothes home to County Waterford. When we returned to Marrakesh, we went to the post office, put our excess bundle of clothes into a cardboard box and wrapped it up. As we pushed our parcel through the grill, we wondered if we'd ever see those clothes again.

Some weeks after our return, the parcel from Marrakesh – tied up with twine and stamped with various exotic marks – arrived home. As I cut the twine, I thought of those Berber women and I wondered if the mysteries of the universe might be unveiled to me if I lived a nomadic life in the desert. Would I taste the wideness, purity, light, silence and emptiness of the night sky in the Sahara if I lived there with the Berbers?

One of the items in the parcel was a leather satchel made of camel skin that we had bought as a present for our mother. It had a long strap, a geometric design on the front and it smelled strongly of camel. Mama put her purse, her handkerchief, a comb and a lipstick into it and wore it, I knew, simply to please us.

It was only when my mother and I later visited an outspoken cousin that the satchel became an issue. After its smoothness was admired, its smell was commented upon – somewhat politely, at first. Tea was made and conversation continued. I sat lost in thought, dreaming of magic carpets and sheiks on their camels in the desert, until our host, trying to be discreet and not offend my mother, asked me in a whisper if I'd mind putting the bag outside the door.

54

Haworth

The village of Haworth in West Yorkshire lived up to all my expectations. It was darkly Gothic; the main street, cobbled and steep, ran wet with runnels of rain. The houses were dour and tall, arching over us like watchful guardians.

I was inspired to take a trip to Haworth in 2006 after seeing *Brontë*, a powerful play by Polly Teale in Dublin's Project Theatre. I wanted to see the village, the moors and the parsonage where this family of such creativity and genius had grown up. RoseAnn, who was equally fascinated by the Brontës – and the fact that they were three sisters – was as eager as me to visit.

It was late September, a weekend when the skies kept opening their sluice-gates to pour bucketfuls of water down on top of us. Each day, on leaving our lodgings to walk on the moors, torrential downfalls would soak us and force us back.

Still, we were determined to reach the ruined farmhouse, Top Withens, which is believed to be the place that inspired Emily Brontë when she wrote *Wuthering Heights*. If we could get to this mythical spot, we were sure we would be at the heart of the moors and the Brontës' wellspring of inspiration.

The farm is about four miles walk from Haworth along a path that crosses over fields, stiles and peaty fenland. As RoseAnn and I set out on our first attempt, sheep stared vacantly at us, hawks flew up suddenly out of heather and soggy moss-covered stones slipped under our feet. On this first attempt, we misgauged the amount of time the hike would take. We could see the deserted homestead dark and forbidding yet seemingly close on the horizon, but before we realised it shadows were lengthening over the marshy ground and we knew we'd have to turn back.

The next day it rained, and a visit to Hatchard & Daughters' booksellers on Haworth's main street was the highlight of our morning. A bell rang as we opened the door and a young woman behind the counter smiled at us in welcome. Within minutes we were happily engrossed and a kind of reverie descended on us as we browsed. My sister and I opened one volume after another, breathing in the musty smell of old books, losing ourselves in a range of titles and covers. The woman at the counter encouraged us to explore further.

When the little bell over the door rang out again, all three of us looked up. A man in rain gear put one foot inside the threshold and asked: 'Do you have a copy of *Mein Kampf*?'

We looked to the twinkling bookseller and wondered what she would say.

'No!' she said.

The man pulled the door shut with a rattle and was gone.

'Ha! Emily Brontë would turn in her grave,' said the bookseller.

I found the last of Mrs Gaskell's seven volumes on *The Life and Works of Charlotte Brontë and Her Sisters* in that shop. The hardback includes portraits and illustrations and a facsimile of the title page of the first edition, as it was when it was published in 1857. Mrs Gaskell wasted no time in writing the biography: Charlotte Brontë had been dead only two years when it came out. The rest of the family were already dead and buried at that stage. Anne was only twenty-nine when she died in 1849. Emily died the year before that at thirty years of age. She died only a few weeks after her brother Branwell. Although ill, she refused to see a doctor or to rest.

We wandered by the parsonage and the church, passing the Black Bull pub on our way, where Branwell drank himself into an early grave. His father slept with him in his final weeks, hoping to nurse him back to health, but the self-destructive drinking had caused too much damage.

The bleakness of the place, the cold and damp of the stone and the loneliness and isolation of the spot, left us grieving for each of the Brontës. The way the light bounced off rain-drenched stone and slate made us emotional and we dreamed about them all, devouring all the books we could find about them.

When we visited the parsonage itself, we saw their little cave-like rooms and narrow beds. Their voices seem to echo off the walls. We saw the room where they sat to sew and write, and the black sofa where it is thought Emily died. Their books are laid out under glass, as is the magnifying glass which was used by their father, Patrick Brontë, in his little room across the hallway. Upstairs we glimpsed the girls' tiny dresses, combs and lace bonnets.

On our last day, a Sunday, the sky was high and clear. We had passed the stone seat where Emily used to sit when it began to rain. We marched on, squelching over the stiles. Then the heavens opened, but still we soldiered on, wanting to endure the cold and wet in memory of the three writers. But finally, when lightning struck and with the water running down our backs and into our shoes, we had to turn back.

We waved goodbye to Top Withens glowering at us in the

distance, almost within touching distance. We went home, thinking how easy it must have been to catch a bad cold in the 1840s and how that could quite possibly have developed into pneumonia and an early death. We consoled ourselves with the fact that we'd truly tasted the full Brontë experience.

55

The Basin Street Visitor

That first night, I waited expectantly for his knock.
Finally, he was there at my door
breathless after running,
He'd got off at the wrong bus stop and hurried to catch
    up with himself.
I let him in
noticing the tightness of his sheepskin coat across his
    chest.
He was like a student outgrowing his clothes,
or a bachelor harkening back to a slimmer time.

I bristled in my bed that night when I heard him coming
    up the stairs,
moving around my house.
Clattering.
My ears pricked, noting each infringement on my
    privacy.

He was in Dublin to attend a weeklong seminar on
    Beckett.
Learned dissertations on the nature of existence was
    sustenance to him.
He loved to talk about emptiness and stillness,
He hungered for it. As did I.

The Basin Street Visitor

In the morning, we rattled around like periwinkles in a
    bucket,
knocking against timber doorjambs,
turning knobs noisily after ablutionary visits to the bath-
    room,
his outrageously bare feet large like paddles on my
    wooden floors.
I left rashers in the fridge for his breakfast
And toffee squares for his tea at night.
He left for Trinity College.
There was no fuss.
He was away all day, coming home late.

He stayed for three days,
He liked to rise early in order to meditate on the futon
    each morning,
His eyes closed, his thoughts suspended in time.
He soaked up the east-rising spring sunshine in the back
    bedroom,
its beautiful creamy light falling like a blessing through
    the window.
He loved the quiet,
the bare walls, the empty stairwell of the house.

But after three nights I said I had to go away,
And that meant he'd have to leave too.
He packed his bag and left the next morning.
He'd find a B&B.
He wasn't perturbed.
Further discussions on Beckett beckoned.
He longed to hear about avant-garde minimalism.

Beyond the Breakwater

I heaved a sigh of relief and finished off the toffee
   squares myself.

He's gone now, Breandán.
I use that bedroom as my office.
The view out the window is a vaulted grey sky over roof-
   tops.

I'm in the Liberties,
If I stand up I can see Guinness's Storehouse,
Off to my right are the Basin Street flats.
And when I think about what to write,
I look out and the shadow of a white cat
walking across the wall outside catches my eye
and a bird,
snug in the heart of long loose lilac branches,
dips in the breeze,
And I remember with a twist of guilt
That it was my uncle who loved this view.

56

Joe Martell

Our house in Waterford city was called 'Corsica'. The three-syllable word appealed to me when I was small. It was a satisfying word to say and I could spell it out easily. I loved the way it sat in cast-iron letters on our gate, all definite and distinct. Cor-si-ca. It was where our great-grandfather, Joe Martell, had come from. It was like a little wayfarer's arrow in those early days: we were here and Corsica was way over beyond, an axis on which to mark a trail.

Joe Martell ran away to sea when he was sixteen. That was back in 1873, a year after a full census was conducted in Ajaccio, the capital of Corsica, which at the time was a bustling fishing port on the western coast of the Mediterranean island. For some reason he didn't want to stay, so he escaped to a life at sea. As I got older, my ideas about my ancestor became a little fanciful – I'd wonder if he ran away because he'd fallen in love with a woman who was forbidden to him by his papa. Perhaps his father, Bastien Martell, a stonemason, had threatened to come after him with a gun for thinking of dishonouring his family in such a way, and so he'd left in a hurry.

What I do know is that he secured a job as a sailor on board a ship and sailed out of Ajaccio, thus becoming a merchant seaman. In time he became a 'bosun' – this is the officer in charge of the deck crew and the ship's deck equipment. On one of his voyages he met Captain William Ryan from Passage

East and the two became friends. They must have been in their twenties when they came to Passage on a holiday, Captain Ryan showing him his home place, where small fishing boats were tied up along the quays in the village, where the houses snuggled in under the cliffs at a narrow stretch in the River Suir before the estuary widens to flow out to open sea.

It was here that Joe Martell met Willie's sister, Mary Ryan. We have a photograph of Mary Ryan wearing a long skirt, standing in the road with her hand raised to shield her eyes from the light. She looks cross, flinty even, as if she's calling someone and is waiting impatiently for that person to come to her. This is in contrast to a photo we have of Joe Martell, who looks dreamy, with a drooping moustache and a slouched soft cloth cap, very much in keeping with the manner of his countrymen back in his native Corsica. His eyes are deep-set under the brim of his cap. Though different, it seems that the two fell in love and were married in 1883 in Crooke church, the grey stone building on the clifftop overlooking the wide expanse of water. They had four daughters – RoseAnn, Maggie, Angela and Mary Ellen, who was the youngest.

My mother, Ena – who was the daughter of Mary Ellen – could clearly remember Joe Martell, even though she was only a little girl when he died. They used to walk along the cockle walk together, chatting away, hand in hand. He had black hair, dark brown eyes and sallow skin. When he got older, he used to make model ships, which he moored against detailed miniature piers, all set against the painted background of the river estuary with detailed 'scapes of Ballyhack, Arthurstown, Duncannon and Cheekpoint. These elaborate seascapes were housed in great display cases made of glass. He used his wife Mary's grey hair for the wisps of smoke coming out of the funnel of the ships.

'You'll be beautiful like your Aunt Madeline when you grow up,' he used to tell my mother when she was small, comparing her to one of his sisters. 'You'll be a lady and ride a horse,' he'd tell her. They used to have great chats. She remembered how he had a funny way of saying certain words, such as 'meeses' instead of mice and 'ices' instead of cream cakes. And we know that he was the first seaman to bring a gramophone home to Passage East from one of his voyages.

It was many years later that RoseAnn and I decided to travel to Corsica. It was a complicated trip that involved flying to Marseilles first, where we felt the lovely heat of the Mediterranean sun on our backs. The next day we caught the ferry and travelled through the summer night towards a distant landmass that loomed ever larger as the dawn came up.

To our knowledge Joe Martell never returned to see his family or the home of his youth. My sister and I were emotional the day we saw the mountains of Corsica in the distance. He had left all of this behind.

As the ferry sailed into the port of Ajaccio, the sun came up and we saw purple and lilac hills wrapped around the ochre and cream-coloured houses of the port. As the ship glided in, the sun burned away the morning mist and the great wide expanse of bay with its corral of white cliffs lay before us. The distant hills were still a sleepy, lilac colour but the sea was a turquoise blue and the houses and hotels of the little town were warm and yellow. RoseAnn and I had lumps in our throats as the boat got closer to the dock.

We were determined to find some links with his past. Maybe we'd find a key to his early life and to his family? We wanted to dig up any trace of him, to see if there was any record of his life.

Our search began as soon as we had docked and checked in to our hotel. Without wasting any time, we headed out towards La Chapelle des Grecs and the local cemetery beyond. It was deathly quiet when we got there in the bright mid-morning. No one was about but we began looking for a Martell plot, wandering through the little narrow lanes that wound themselves between the large tombs and lavish burial chambers.

We peered at the family names and at the sad framed photographs of the deceased. Nervously, we squeezed through half-open gates into forgotten, overgrown parts. It was an eerie place in the white sunshine with the cicadas clacking away. It was still, ancient and deserted. In the end, Le Cimetière des Sept Familles yielded no clues. We felt rejected as we walked back towards the centre of Ajaccio.

Over the coming days we went through the census records at the national archives, trawling through dusty columns of names. With our broken French, we asked bemused natives for directions. They looked sceptically at us. Perhaps they wondered why we were not going to the beach or to trek in the mountains. We visited the Maritime Museum where one man hunched his shoulders, lifted his eyebrows and said with a Gallic flourish: 'Il est difficile le trouver, comme une aiguille dans une meule de foin.'

'Oui,' we said, nodding our heads in weariness, just about grasping his meaning – which had to do with our search being difficult, like finding a needle in a haystack. 'C'est vrai,' I responded, giving my few Gallic words a spin of their own.

That time, we left without unearthing any living link with Joe Martell or his family (due to a misunderstanding we had only trawled through one-third of the 1872 census, so we hadn't even found his name) and yet we did feel as if we'd uncovered something. We both realised there was something odd about the place, the sun, the stone, the shade and the locals. In the old part of the town it struck us both very forcibly that there was something familiar about Corsica. In Le Vieux Port d'Ajaccio we walked the narrow streets and we knew what it reminded us of. The smells, the cool evenings, the shade-darkened corners, the sunlit concrete, even the faces of the people seemed to remind us of Passage, our childhood holiday idyll.

Le Vieux Port d'Ajaccio was just like our mother's village. It had the same sea-going vibe, the same breezy aspect, the same narrow, curved streets with their pockets of coolness and warmth. The yellow stones in the sunshine seemed white, reminiscent of the whitewashed houses in Passage.

As we left, we were determined we'd return. It made us smile to think that our great-grandfather – the salty mariner who had run away to sea – had found a home away from home in Waterford. It seemed as if he had fulfilled his childhood dreams of going to sea and, rather than escaping, he had run towards his fate and made his home in Passage East.

57

Rome

When RoseAnn and I visited Rome some years ago, we decided to visit our Aunt Máire's grave. She'd been a teaching nun in Rome for many years, a member of the Sacred Heart of Mary Order. She had taught at the order's school, Marymount. We wanted to pay our respects. We'd forego the Colosseum and the Trevi Fountain until the second day of our visit and we'd search instead for the convent graveyard on the Via Nomentana.

I remembered Auntie Máire as a soft-spoken woman with glasses and short grey hair. She was not without vanity as she would never allow her sister to claim that she was younger than her and she used to ask my mother to put a set in her hair with the electric rollers when she was home on her biannual holiday. She was usually dressed in various shades of navy or grey – always blouses, cardigans and sensible skirts – the days of the full habit and the wimple that she had worn in earlier decades were long gone at that stage.

She had a steely quality about her too, a quiet steady look that I remember. It was the all-knowing look of someone who is used to teaching teenage girls. Generally, we kept out of her way for fear she might ask about our spiritual wellbeing or our religious intentions. But she used to bring us lovely presents – beach bags, sun hats and bracelets – all imbued with the summer colours of Roman stalls. She knew what we'd like. And yet, a sighting of Auntie Máire on the horizon could often occasion a mad dash out of view as we were convinced she might ask us if we'd ever considered the idea of entering the convent.

Sr Alphonsus – or Sr Máire Foley as she was known in later years – had only been a teenager when she entered the convent. Born in 1913, she was barely sixteen when she left Ireland to join the Sacre Coeur Order in the United States. Family lore has it that she played the violin as the ship pulled away from the quay, her father, Dan Foley, waving her off. She was his third eldest. It was a life-changing step to take. She was not allowed home – even for her father's funeral in 1937 – nor for many years after that.

Her time in New York's Tarrytown, where she made her First Profession of vows in 1933, was followed by a stint in California, then France and finally Italy, where she was based for many years, until her death in 1984 when she was seventy years of age. We knew she was a teacher and a principal at the order's secondary school, where many famous people sent their children. And so we set out to find the convent and the little graveyard on Rome's Via Nomentana.

The streets were deserted as we headed off. It was a bank holiday in Italy that day and it was the middle of winter. We were delighted when we found that long, leafy boulevard. When we discovered a little stone church just off the boulevard we felt confident we were close, as there was a small cemetery behind it. We couldn't be sure it was the correct place, of course, but with a high level of hope we walked between the slabs of stones, feeling like emissaries from old Erin's Isle, bringing the family's love to our exiled relative. The dry chill gave the tombs and the dusty railings, the crosses and little plinths an extra frisson of finality, but we were sure that if we could only identify her grave we'd be able to commune in some way with Auntie Máire's soul.

But there were no inscriptions that we could decipher. We could find no clues in the Italian wording or the Roman numerals on the little slabs. We didn't know what else to do. Of course, we didn't dare phone the convent on the Via Nomentana. After years of maintaining our distance from nuns, we had an inbuilt reluctance to engage with religious communities of any kind. So after an hour or two, we went back out through the little church onto the wide sloping thoroughfare of the Via Nomentana.

The city was quiet in the twilight. There was a hush about the evening. It felt like a Sunday. Very few cars passed and we were tired after the time we'd spent wandering amongst the dead. We shivered, feeling the night was full of portent. We crossed the wide residential street and began the trek in the direction of the city centre.

In the dimly lit gloom, we both looked back ruefully, sad that we hadn't found Auntie Máire's grave, and that's when we saw her – the nun, as if floating above the hedge, her long wimple unmistakable, her silhouette lit within the domed awning of a fanlight. It seemed like an unnaturally large head.

We gripped one another, terrified, and walked on quickly, not sure what we had seen. Was it a larger than life etching of a nun's head in an alcove? Had it hovered there over the hedge? Had it followed us?

As we passed, the ghostly vision seemed to disappear. All of a sudden it was gone out of view. It was as if she had been a figment of our imagination. (In hindsight I realise it was only a large etching of a nun's wimpled head, framed and lit within the fanlight of a doorway.) But the momentary nature of her appearance spooked us and we started to run, as if for our lives. We ran until we were breathless. We ran the length of the Via Nomentana, terrified, and it would be many years before we returned.

58

The Diary of a Social Columnist

In due course, after working as a reporter on education, property and news stories over a number of years in *The Irish Times*, I was asked to write the newspaper's social column. It was 1999, just before the dawn of the new millennium. I was excited and pleased to be asked. It meant that I would be attending important events in the arts world, covering all aspects of the literary, theatrical, musical, artistic, orchestral and celebratory life of the city. It also meant that I'd have a picture by-line and that I'd have the opportunity to write descriptive and more detailed passages, or 'colour' as it's known in journalistic circles.

The column was an established element of the paper and was called 'On the Town'. It comprised a full page each Saturday on the back page of the paper's weekend supplement and entailed writing about eight separate stories, most of which were accompanied by colour photographs. In all, I was a social columnist with the paper for nine years in Dublin.

In due course I learned that it meant attending a relentless stream of social and cultural events, which I had to record and describe. My main focus was to ensure that the stories I recorded were of interest and value to readers. My routine generally began each evening around 5 p.m. when I'd leave the offices of *The Irish Times* on D'Olier Street and head off into the evening, my pen and notebook in my pocket, my energy levels cranked up, my best walking shoes laced up tightly and a small haversack hanging off my back for ease of movement. (Although strappy stilettos were the order of the day for many of the fashionable women who attended the openings and launch parties that I was sent to cover, my fashion statement was that a strong pair of walking shoes would serve me better.) Even though I was invited to glitzy, glamorous parties, the country girl in me never let me forget that I'd be dashing between events on foot and that being well shod in a proper pair of flat shoes was a necessity.

My beat was generally Dublin's city centre, which stretched from the top of O'Connell Street across the Liffey to the top of Stephen's Green. For a frantic three to four hours, I'd wind my way through the throngs of invited guests at particular parties and functions, gathering information as I went, never to be deflected from my sole objective – to gather enough detail and data to allow me write up my weekly column. I attended a couple of gala events over three and sometimes four nights a week. I'd file my copy on Thursday evening or after midnight on Friday morning. It would appear in the paper on Saturday.

Of an evening I might dash up to Nassau Street to Waterstones for a book launch. I'd take notes during the speeches, jot down all the details, collect the names of those present and speak to the author, the publisher and the individual who had launched the book. I'd liaise with the photographer and then I'd be off, hightailing it up to the Olympia Theatre or perhaps the Project Theatre in Temple Bar for the opening of a new play. Here again I'd squeeze myself through the gathering, greet delighted and excited partygoers and, like a bee gathering honey, I'd buzz from person to person, collecting material.

Usually my demeanour was of the pragmatic variety: I often reminded myself of a garda on his/her beat. I'd ask the name, occupation, rank and current plans of those guests I met. I had no time for, nor did I appreciate, any levity or false information. With my gimlet eye trained on the interviewee, my pen poised and my patience in check, I'd wait until he or she was fully composed before proceeding. Time was always of the essence and getting to a venue on time was always my top priority. So I was pleasant but efficient, moving all the time, jotting down notes as I went. Earnest and unblinking, I only bestowed a limited amount of air kisses on those I met! Not much alcohol – no matter how much champagne was being quaffed and offered – used to pass my lips while I was on duty, as I was a no-nonsense sort of diarist.

This had all coincided with the Celtic Tiger years, when delicious canapés, glasses of Chablis and flutes of Veuve Clicquot, strobe lights, high-end fashion and fabulous events were the order of the day; where style, charm, brilliance and vivacity were *de rigueur*. Sometimes I'd ask myself if I was supposed to be enjoying myself while at these events, but then a puritanical streak would quickly reassert itself and I'd remind myself that I was working, that this was my job and not an opportunity to party until the small hours.

Of course, at times I did enjoy myself; I made many new friends and I met famous and fabulous people – Angelina Jolie, John McGahern, John B. Keane, Yoko Ono, Pierce Brosnan, Louis Le Brocquy, Jonathan Miller, Edna O'Brien. I usually made my way to the most celebrated individuals in the room to ask a couple of questions. Sometimes it was a job that required a thick skin and a certain degree of brazenness.

I was witness to the unveiling of amazing works of art – in theatre, literature, music, painting, dance and sculpture. I grew to appreciate the strength of artistic life in the city and beyond as I was sometimes sent to cover cultural events in places such as Kilkenny, Galway, Cork and even London. I knew my way around the galleries, theatres, bookshops, museums, halls, emporiums and happening venues of the city. I was *on the town* and a regular at events in the Irish Museum of Modern Art, the Gaiety, the National Concert Hall, the National Gallery, the Abbey, the Gate and the Hugh Lane Gallery.

Some people go into a religious order to contemplate life and the meaning of human existence. Some prefer to live in Tibet for seven years. My nine-year vocation, however, involved me being a chronicler of the arts scene in the capital.

At night, after whirling my way around the cultural hotspots of the city where creativity, artistic endeavour and dramatic out-pourings were the order of the day, I'd return to my small house and sit in silence, wondering if it had all really happened.

Return

59

The Missing Painting

My mother used to sit at the kitchen table at home and paint away to her heart's content. She'd lose herself in the work and forget about time. It was only when my father stuck his head in around 6 p.m., wondering about the tea, that she'd realise how late it was.

She had always pottered with art – driftwood, shell pictures, rockeries in the garden, masks for Halloween, bespoke knitting designs and the like. She had always been making things and taking photographs, but it was only when we had all flown the coop that she had enough time to take up a paintbrush. It was then that her life as an artist took off in earnest. In each painting she seemed to capture something of herself, of her own youth growing up on the mouth of the Suir in Passage East – there is a certain timeless energy, a stillness and an innocence in every picture.

Her paintings of boats, piers, moonscapes, gardens, land-scapes, seagulls and cliffs hang all around our house in Ring – they are a tangible link to my mother and her individuality. They are not abstract but detailed and lyrical works. They are paintings that tell stories; like a poem by Walter de la Mare, they are full of expectation and stark wonder.

And so it happened that one Sunday morning some years ago, when I was at home, I saw that my mother was all a-flutter when we told her that local painter, the great Mick Mulcahy, was on his way over to the house. Mick is an expressionist painter whose work hangs in homes and galleries around the world. Having heard something about Mama's painting, he wanted to have a look at her work for himself. She welcomed him in and Mick set about inspecting the paintings. She smiled nervously as she waited for his verdict.

'Magnificent,' he declared, growing more effusive as he studied each successive painting. My mother beamed with delight.

'Will you do a swap? Will you give me one of yours – in exchange for one of mine?' he suggested. And my mother agreed, honoured to be recognised in such a fashion.

'Pick whichever one you'd like,' she told him. So Mick chose a painting that was hanging in our hall at the time, a medium-sized painting that I particularly liked – a raw visceral scene of a jagged rock with three seagulls swooping across it out towards a turquoise sea. Mick went away with it under his arm and my mother was pleased. They were friends from then on, both respectful of the other, each recognising a kindred spirit.

Years passed and in time my mother had to stop painting as the debilitating illness that claimed her prevented her from holding the brush. But when she passed away in 2011 we had her paintings, each one more precious than the last.

Yet I often wondered about the painting she had given to Mick Mulcahy. Like a special memory, I missed that particular one and felt its loss. After Mick moved away from the area, his former studio – a great shed at the side of the road – fell into ruin. I used to pass this hulk of a building with its corrugated iron roof and nettles growing out of its slabbed entrance and wonder if he'd taken my mother's painting with him or if he'd forgotten it and left it there in the damp, thrown in the corner to rot from mildew. I never felt that I could ask him for the painting, as I had no claim on it, so I came to accept that the painting was lost forever – until recently, that is.

I was at a funeral, sympathising with a neighbour over the death of his own mother when he mentioned it out of the blue.

'You know I have a painting your mother did,' he said. 'She did a swap with Mick Mulcahy and he gave it to me to mind.' He explained how he used to go into the shed where Mick worked. 'The painting,' he said, 'it caught my eye the minute I went in and I asked Mick who had done it. Ena Foley, he told me. He said he had done a swap for it and that he had to give your mother one of his.'

I smiled at the idea that the painting still existed. Páid, my neighbour, offered to give it back to me but I declined. On another day he called to insist again that we have it. In the end, we brought him in and showed him how many of our mother's paintings we had hanging on the walls. We told him that it was enough to know he had it and that it was safe.

He was happy then. The story had come full circle. My mother's painting is in his house still, there in the warmth, appreciated and on view. She'd have been delighted to know that. And to know that Mick, her fellow artist, had taken good care of it all along. I should have known he would.

60

Theatre Royal

The great tenor, Frank Ryan, sang on the stage of the Theatre Royal on the Mall in Waterford city. Like Caruso, he was a naturally gifted singer who sprang from the land, untrained but brilliant and bursting with talent, just waiting to be unleashed on the world in the 1930s.

He died in the early 1960s before he was captured on film, but in 2008, I – along with my sister RoseAnn and a film crew – set about recreating a moment from his career for a documentary we were making about him.

We'd started making documentaries together when I was still working as a journalist in Dublin. However, in 2008 I applied for and was awarded a voluntary redundancy package which was on offer in *The Irish Times*. I wanted to write full-time, so in due course I moved home to Ring. RoseAnn, who wanted to continue making documentaries, also decided to return home. Soon we began to carve out a living as TV documentary-makers, making programmes for the Irish-language station TG4.

Telling the story of Frank Ryan was one of our earliest programmes. He'd been a butcher, a farmer and an internationally successful tenor. How could TG4 resist the idea? We were duly commissioned to make a half-hour documentary about him.

RoseAnn, as director, decided to hire the Theatre Royal for an afternoon and ask a local actor, Hank Regan, to come and play the part of the great singer. She asked him to mime the singing of 'Mo Chuisle, Your Sweet Voice is Calling,' and then to bow to an imaginary, rapturous audience.

The beautifully restored Victorian auditorium, horseshoe-shaped and intimate, was eerily dark and receptive when we arrived. My job was to climb up through the narrow passageways and ladders to the gantry behind the stage and to man the switch that would both release and raise the red velvet stage curtain as was needed.

There was hush as the lights came on, throwing a lovely glow over Hank. As he mimed, I waited for a quick call on the mobile to tell me to release the curtains. It came and I pressed the switch. The weights in the curtain's hem brought them to a halt with a satisfying drop. I did it again and again, as the filming continued. I waited in the quiet and looked down from above. All the world was a stage.

I was free to dream as I sat in the gantry that day. Under the roof of the old theatre, I began to listen to the ghosts of thespians whispering all around me. I imagined the productions, the smothered laughter, the tippy-toe dashes behind the wings, the divas and the stars; I imagined all the lives that were tied up in that space. I'm not sure whether it was the intoxication of those small darkened corners, the precariousness of the platform I was standing on, the maniacal nature of our endeavour to create a sense of Frank Ryan's life on stage, or the sheer joy of being at play in a theatre – maybe it was a combination of all these factors – but being in the gantry of the Theatre Royal created a powerful sense of giddiness in me that afternoon. As I released the curtains again, I tried to smother my laughter. Between takes, I boogied up and down, and I imagined myself flying down to the footlights, airborne like a trapeze artist.

Theatre Royal

As I tried to stifle my giddiness, my own solo moment on the stage of the Theatre Royal many years earlier came back to me. As a child, I had played the part of a guardian angel in a school play for Féile na Scoile. I had been dressed in white to my toes and I wore wings that were made with wire hangers and covered in white mesh edged with silver sequins and held on with elastic bands. I was to sing solo. My arms held aloft, I glided on and sang about how I would protect 'the two little orphans, a boy and a girl who were lost and alone in the snow'.

I remember my five-year-old self on stage that night and how the footlights blinded me as I looked out at the audience. I can still recall the energy, the electricity of that moment when I made my debut on the Waterford stage. I recall the combined intake of breath as I backed away and how I sidestepped nicely to avoid the upright piano that had threatened to obstruct my exit.

Then I remembered Miriam, my younger sister, on the same stage of the Theatre Royal as a seven-year-old, conducting her class in a performance of 'How Much is that Doggy in the Window?' With her back to us, her long blond hair shimmering in the footlights, she kept a steady beat with her baton and we all gloried in the emphatic rhythm and skill of her one-two-three, one-two-three hand movements. How proud my parents were.

In a few short years we had left Lower Newtown in Waterford, but my pulse still races when I see Rice Bridge spanning the River Suir on the way into the city or when I travel up around Reginald's Tower and along the Mall. My heart quickens when I hear the lovely flat Waterford accent.

The tug is still there, the tug of that place and those days when the Theatre Royal was a focal point for us in primary school and when we were both thrilled and terrified to be stepping out onto a city stage on a night filled with firsts.

61

The Premiere

Excitement began to mount as the time of the guests' arrival drew closer. Even Pingin, the dog, picked up on the air of anticipation in the house in Baile na nGall, barking and jumping up on the armchairs.

We had screwed two hooks into our sitting room ceiling and hung a pole. Then we draped a white sheet over this to create a screen. It was perfect. The homemade canvas seemed to lift the room onto another plane. Suddenly I knew how the Lumière Brothers must have felt. It would be a premiere like no other. Our sitting room was not large but we crammed enough chairs in to turn it into a mini picture house. It was to be our own Cinema Paradiso.

We moved the couches back and put the sideboard into a corner where we assembled drinks, glasses and nibbles in readiness for the party. We hung fairy lights from the lamps and the paintings. Outside we rolled out a strip of red carpet that RoseAnn, who was the film's director and its main instigator, had bought especially for the occasion in M. J. Curran's shop in Dungarvan.

We'd invited many of the participants who had taken part in our documentary. Most of them were coming. We borrowed a projector from an engineering company in Cork and we'd run the film to make sure everything was working.

It was a warm, balmy night in September 2009 when cocktail

dresses and off-the-shoulder tops seemed just the ticket. It was a night for a party and it was just getting dark when the cars began to pull up.

I took up my position with a camera and stood behind the red rope we'd hung by the edge of the carpet. I was at the ready à la paparazzi to snap the 'celebs' as they arrived.

They parked in our driveway and on the road outside. It was our own Boulevard de la Croisette; Cannes had come to Baile na nGall. When Carol Anne Hennessy from Midleton, who played the part of Molly Keane in a few short scenes in our film, arrived with her mother, Angela, I asked them to wave for the cameras as they walked up to our front door.

It was my recent reading of a new book about Molly Keane by her elder daughter, Sally Phipps, that brought it all back to me – making that documentary about the great Anglo-Irish writer, the creator of the masterpiece and Booker-shortlisted novel *Good Behaviour*. It had been a thrilling experience, possibly one of the best films my sister RoseAnn and I ever made; but by far and away the best part of having the world premiere of our half hour film was that we celebrated it at home that night with our parents. Our mother's health was failing and our father's memory was going. There was a sense of fragility about their presence with us that night. Each of us – Miriam, RoseAnn and I – felt time was running out. We knew we had to commemorate and cherish the time we had left with them.

On the night, Sally herself appeared with her husband, the late George Phipps, and her sister, Virginia, also came along with her husband, Kevin Brownlow, who won a lifetime achievement Oscar the following year for his work in silent film. They all arrived, the girls bearing pots of jam, bottles of wine and homegrown flowers. Their friend and neighbour, Tony Gallagher, a boatman and sometime film-maker, came too, smiling and eager to see how his own contribution to our documentary would appear. Neighbours and friends came too.

We packed in, introducing each one to our elderly parents. Then we took our seats, turned off the lights and the projector hummed into life. Immediately the lively music of long ago seduced us along with Molly's lovely open face and her clipped upper-crust accent.

We were well into her story when the projector had a little upset and the film stuttered to an end. On went the lights. No need to panic, RoseAnn assured us. But my father, hemmed in on the couch at the far end of the room, stood up and made a rush towards the door. Thinking he'd been caught short and needed to get to the bathroom, I pushed bodies aside in my panic, knowing that time was of the essence.

'This way, Daddy,' I said, whispering, 'the bathroom is this way.'

'What? No,' he said, refusing my arm. 'I want to buy a drink. Where's the bar?'

I smiled apologetically at those who were seated and brought him to the sideboard, loving his irrepressible sense of occasion and his redoubtable ability to maintain the social niceties.

It was a night full of memories like that, all shot through with the delight of having my parents present. And I imagined Molly Keane herself, who adored parties, scooting along on her way towards us, as described by Sally in *Molly Keane: A Life*: 'driving in her Morris Minor and (later) Renault 5s, she was like a lone sailor on a small craft, watchful, all senses on the alert, open to adventure'.

62

Ardkeen Visit

My mother and father are in bed smiling at me like bold children. Tucked up, lying side by side, they watch me as I leave the room. I stand by the door and their eyes, expectant and loving, rest on me, their eldest.

Her eyes twinkle. 'Hands off the serge,' she says to him, pretending outrage, smiling all the while as she removes his hand from hers. There's a spark between them still and I'm caught off guard. They are entertaining me with that oft-repeated line of fey authority – a phrase that had been common in Waterford when they'd both worked there many decades before: it had once been uttered by a draper's assistant with notions of superiority in a shop in the city after a customer dared touch some expensive fabric on the counter.

As I go to leave the bedroom, my father calls me back, worried. 'Where's Ena?' he wants to know.

Lying beside him, her eyes dim with disappointment, my mother discovers what it is to be alone.

'She's there beside you,' I say.

He lifts his head and looks. 'Ena, is that you?' he says, delight and relief flooding his voice.

Soon after this incident I take my father to Ardkeen, the hospital in Waterford, to be reviewed by the doctor and his team. Again and again as we drive towards Waterford I have to explain where we are going.

'You have an appointment with the doctor,' I tell him.

When we arrive and the kind Dr Hassan sits down to talk to my father, he looks again to me for reassurance. 'Is this the doctor?' he asks. 'Yes,' I say. 'Will he help me to … to exist,' he wonders, searching for the correct word.

Once, when I'd been a student, the mediocrity of life at home felt like a rash all over me. However, that was some time ago now. I no longer railed against suffocating days of regular meals and bright fires. There was no more angst and there was no more pulling against him. There was only the slow, inexorable beat of days moving towards a sad diminishment and an end that will leave an empty space by the fire, a cold bed and a free weekend to loll and drift. The weekly schedule of shopping and cooking will be gone and we will swing away in confusion, heartbroken and weightless, lonely and released, dangling free in the empty days. I harden myself to it before it has happened.

When we were small, we sat around my father on the strand and he told us a story about a mermaid. We listened, mesmerised, as the sun warmed our backs and the tide slipped over the rocks, pulling the seaweed every which way. My mother boiled a kettle on a little hill of stones and driftwood that she'd built on the sand. It was a day of magic. We have all forgotten the details of the story but not the spell it cast over us.

All our childhood we were three little girls, little princesses, washed in soft sudsy soap, dressed in fresh cotton, fed on boiled new potatoes, Batchelor's beans, kippers and smoked haddock. We did their bidding, little goslings, chirruping and escaping the nest occasionally, but always reeled back in with them clucking and admonishing us, feeding us and admiring us, worshipping us.

What a happy household.

The tables have turned. They move like tortoises now. They have handed the reins over to us. I stay at home more and more as it's clear I am needed here. We help them wash and dress. Now, there is the chance to caress my father's cheek, to rifle in his manly-smelling pockets and help him transfer his wallet, keys, handkerchief and comb from one pair of trousers to another. I help my mother close the clasp of her gold watch around her rail-thin wrist. I pull on her socks and wait to carry her handbag for her.

'Where are we?' my father queries later that night. 'What's the name of this place?'

'You are at home in Baile na nGall,' I tell him. I don't remind him of its meaning, which translates as Home of the Strangers.

'Are you sure?' he asks, unconvinced, unhappy with my answer. He's still at sea. I begin to take my leave and kiss him goodnight. When my sister pops in to say goodnight he has rephrased his question in order to elicit a more revealing response.

'Where do you think you are?' he asks her, placing gentle stresses on the more significant second person pronouns. It is a clever philosophical conundrum. She tells him he is at home. She gives him the exact address and reassures him that it is his house. But we both look at each other doubtfully, each of us questioning our certainty. We shake our heads wryly. Dada, seeing us pause, sensing our momentary reluctance to commit, seems pleased. After that, he settles down quietly.

A stranger called to our house recently, lost and weary. I gave him tea and an éclair. He sat and tried to regain his composure but we could see he was struggling with his own inner demons. He'd just cycled fifteen miles to meet his brother who lived nearby but no one was at home. My father, sitting at the fire, his native, irrepressible sociability coming to the fore, asked him his name and where he was from.

'I'm sorry,' he said then. 'I don't mean to ask personal questions. I'm in the way. Don't mind me at all.' The stranger looked at him, sweat still forming on his forehead. It was an odd meeting. They were both lost, both apologising. I took my chance to rub my father's cheek and tell him he was in his own house and that he was in no one's way.

>⤙⤚<

The days are full of remembering here. It's like being bathed in the long shadows of a dying sun. I was seven or eight when I went through my wild stage. I remember one evening when I caused my mother great upset. I didn't mean to, of course. I was just happy and I forgot to come home. I remember looking down on the little holiday village of Passage East from the hill that hung overhead. I could see tiny people walking from one corner to another, disappearing into the maze of little streets and then re-emerging onto another square or quay. In my memory, I see my mother, in an aerial Fellini-esque type scene, running out of Gran's house, calling me, racing across the square, past the pump, down the lane, looking for me frantically. I waved and shouted but she never heard me.

'Look, Mama,' I called.

I had no sense of wrongdoing. I was blithely following my heart, playing with a couple of boys and girls. After the great hill, we climbed down again and went out in a canoe, out beyond the breakwater. We glided like angels over the water through a sparkling arc of light. It was late when I arrived home, replete and exhausted.

My mother shook me. I was never to do anything like that again, she told me, and truly, I haven't. My father must have been at work that day but I'm sure he was told about my boldness and the danger I'd been in. Sometimes I wonder if that escapade wasn't a dream time.

Together my parents created a pattern day after day that shaped and regulated our days. Sometimes I imagine him leaving for work in Waterford, suited and shaved, kissed and waved off. 'Slán leat,' she may have said, or maybe she whispered something more private. Then we'd leave for school, life stretching out ahead of us, days of blue skies. No radio, no noise, only my mother's voice calling in Irish to go safely – 'Slán libh.' Her voice seemed to echo down the street. Her right arm upraised, her left holding the gate closed. These distant, distinct mornings shimmered as we made our way across and up the hill to concrete yards, tiled corridors and nuns with beads and black rushing robes.

The mornings don't seem as newly minted any more but my mother still stands at the front door, her arm raised like a stick to wave me off whenever I leave. They stand together now in the doorway and smile, warning me to take my time. I pull away in my car, watching them in the rear-view mirror. They are framed at the hall door, and are again in my mirror, doubly captured in a freeze-frame, poised for a camera shot. She is in front of him, smaller. How long more, I wonder. And I accelerate up the hill until the house is out of view and all the mornings in between back then and now, all the partings, all the stillness, is a pattern, a thread of time, of light. They are there now, but their image fades quickly.

It has been over fifty years. The hours are drawing in. They sleep longer and wake less. They slip into a snooze by the fire.

Ardkeen Visit

In his suit recently, preparing for a celebratory birthday meal, I helped comb his hair.

'Where's your mother?' he asked, full of devilment. 'I want to ask her if she'd marry me.' I pointed to the room where my mother was being prepared like a young bride for an outing. In the midst of having her hair done and her make-up applied, there was a little knock at the bedroom door.

'Ena, are you there?' He opened the door tentatively, his foot on the threshold of my sister's inner sanctum.

'Will you marry me?' he asked, his eyes full of fun.

'I will,' she answered, smiling with delight, looking at him, handsome in his tailored jacket. Her eyes danced and so did his.

The passion is there still.

Not that things were always perfect. For one thing, my father had a bad track record with gifts. Once, he brought her fine strong scissors from Cork as a present. Although it was something she needed, my mother did not view this in a favourable light. As a gift, it was an unflinching failure. Another resounding flop was the long-playing record of brass-band marches that he brought home to her; my mother let him know it was not acceptable. She remained cross with him, even though my father was at a loss to understand what was wrong with this glorious vinyl offering.

He sometimes asks about friends and family who are long dead. 'Is Breandán dead?' he checks. 'I don't remember that at all,' he claims, angry and disappointed at the discovery that his brother has gone. He often wonders about his mother, too, though she has been dead almost fifty years.

'Where is she?' he asks. 'I don't remember my mother dying,' he declares, and for a moment he slumps, overcome with the grief and confusion of losing her. It is the same with all his relations and friends who pop into his head from time to time.

'What?' he says, upset and ashamed that he is only finding out now, that he has not sympathised with the family. 'But I never knew he was dead. No one told me.'

Often overruled by a houseful of women, he created corners that were out of bounds to us. The desk was a no-go area. 'That's my desk,' he used to declare defiantly. Now I riffle through it, happily clearing and organising his papers, aware of my trespassing fingers combing through documents that he valued, folded away and labelled – bank statements, lotto numbers, valuations from auctioneers, passports, medical records and diaries where he wrote down the sayings and stories he heard that appealed to him.

He is more biddable and easier now than before. There are no more territorial stand-offs. 'Don't touch anything in that shed,' he'd warn, forestalling any intentions we had of clearing out the great maw of tangled things where the coal was kept, along with all the garden tools, his lobster pots and fishing gear, the old tins of paint and any bits of building materials that might have been left behind. Before we began to reclaim this dominion, it was his place, his terrain. Dark, dusty and cluttered, it was full of broken things that he dreamed of re-using, of resurrecting in some way when he had the time to fix and release their potential. I remember my mother pulling his leg gently when he rescued the rusty rim and handle of an old tin bucket. 'I might use that someday to harness a goat,' he told her, trying to conceal the laugh in his own eyes. We never did get a goat but he looked out the window that day and imagined tethering such a stubborn animal to the hedge.

Ardkeen Visit

'Daddy, did you shave yet?' I ask him, and the question will worry him for the entire morning, taking root in his mind. He will return again and again and ask me if he has shaved. I will stroke his cheek and tell him that he has, or that he has missed a bit under his chin.

In all his working life he rarely stayed late in bed, unless he was very sick. Now, he loves to have his breakfast taken up to him. Is it the petting he never got as a child? This softer, quieter man is my father too and we are getting to cosy up to him like we did on the strand long ago. We have almost forgotten the energetic, bellowing man who slammed doors in frustration and ended up losing most domestic battles, and in the end, didn't mind at all. That man is harder to find nowadays.

63

Ballast

In all the photographs I come across
I am leaning in to him,
Like an old wheel standing up against a wall,
His arm draped around my shoulders.
We often posed together like that.
And I recall the solidity of him,
He was like ballast in a boat,
He'd not stir,
He was steady as she goes,
On that garden seat.

64

Christmas by the Graves

That first year after my mother died there was a palpable draw to those flat green plots. We couldn't resist. I suppose the quiet enclave had become a place of familiarity to us after Mama passed away. It was my sister RoseAnn and her friend Kathleen next door, both of them grieving for their mothers, who sent word out that we'd meet there in the graveyard to remember and say the rosary.

It was probably the emptiness we craved when we wandered up through the graves to wait for the others. It was almost 3 p.m. on Christmas Eve, a time when all the shops were still open and shopping was at its peak.

But like a little miracle, a raggle-taggle bunch of people began appearing. We watched when a car stopped outside on the road and a young man got out. He sauntered up as if he wasn't quite sure if he was coming or not. But, forgetting his jacket and with just a set of keys jangling from his hand, he kept coming. Next a mother and her daughter came along, both buttoned up and gloved, booted and scarfed; it was clear they were determined to attend.

We had nightlights in jam jars in readiness for everyone and the process of getting the candles alight and keeping them lit helped to diffuse the shyness, the communal embarrassment, and instead reminded us that we *wanted* to be in that forgotten, sad place on that happiest of days. A handful of couples, a sprinkling of families and one or two on their own also arrived.

At 3 p.m. we drew in near to the priest for the opening lines of the 'Coróin Mhuire' and the first decade of the rosary. It began quietly, the Irish prayers wafting across the cemetery, but it soon seemed as if we were all stepping out onto a sonic tightrope, moving as one, going from one bead to the next, from one 'Hail Mary' to the next, bound together by that old prayer. The sounds seemed to swell and take possession of us, until we came to the end of the first decade on a communal breath, inhaling and exhaling.

When someone else took it up, we were off again: *Go mbeannaí duit, a Mhuire, atá lán de ghrásta, tá an Tiarna id 'tochar, is beannaithe tú idir mhnáibh agus is beannaithe toradh do bhroinn Íosa.* (Hail Mary, full of grace, the Lord is with thee, blessed art thou amongst women and blessed is the fruit of thy womb Jesus.)

Each time we answered together. We recited it in a rush, as if we were running out of breath, galloping up into the clouds: *A Naomh Mhuire, a mháthair Dé, guigh orainn anois agus ar uair ár mbáis. Amen.* (Holy Mary, mother of God, pray for us now and at the hour of our death. Amen.)

Praying through Irish seemed to power us like a dynamo. It felt as if we were sending a signal up into the heavens.

We stayed at it like that and when we came to the end of another ten, we seemed to have grown into the calmness. And though we flinched in the rain, and though the ghostly sound of our voices was blown by the wind over the headstones and away out to sea, we stood our ground and stayed the course. And the sky, grey and lowering, darkened stealthily, until it had wrapped us up in a grey, numbing nothingness. It was the quietness all around that drew us down into the clay and stilled us.

When we finished, Miriam suggested we sing a verse of 'Adeste Fideles' and after a timid start we were off. And with the Latin came the powerful sense of all those past Christmases. As we sang that hymn to hope, it seemed we were all together again in a chapel long ago, voices bursting with exuberance and my father singing as if to lift the roof: *Venite adoremus, Dominum.*

And so it's happened every year since, where we do a shy shuffle up to that spot, to stand in the cold in the middle of the graveyard, to pray for all of fifteen minutes and sing. Afterwards we walk carefully away, as if we might spill something en route back to the car. Christmas wouldn't be Christmas now without those cold grey moments by the grave.

65

Respite

Down the corridor at the nurses' station many of the patients in Buxton chairs were gathered in a glut, pulled in to the low desk as if they were protesting at some airline counter and would begin to wave their tickets shortly. Their animated conversations filled the air. Some nodded their heads, some rocked back and forth; others gesticulated and questioned as if their lives depended on an answer. It gladdened my heart to see them all there as near as they could get to the seat of power, the nurses' station.

One man, wrestling with the buckle of a seat belt at the side of his chair, proffered it to me as if it was a key or a wallet.

'This is my fork,' he said in clear, enunciated words, looking intently at me.

'I'll put it in here for you,' I said and buckled him in. He seemed pleased as I stepped away.

Lost in a darkened world of their own, speaking truths full of wisdom and woe, they linger and live on into their eighties and nineties, men and women who are confused, uttering nonsensical mutterings, their limbs shrivelled and frail.

A nurse sat at the other side of the counter, writing and answering an occasional question. She glanced at me in a distracted way and we smiled, sane beings in a world of confused souls. She was relaxed as she worked and chatted to them, knowing they were safe under her care and unable to wander off.

Respite

'They don't know where they are,' she said to me as I passed down the corridor.

I turned in to my father's ward. He was staying in the local community hospital for a couple of days' respite for both himself and for us at home. He had gone downhill rapidly after the death of our mother. On the day of her funeral in July 2011, we saw his spirit drop dramatically. Dementia seemed to envelop him even as we led him to the open grave on that lonely morning.

I busied myself at his side. There at his bedside I could see how the day swelled for him, growing into a lonely echoing space that was foreign and full of quiet. It felt like I'd abandoned him and that he was quietly accepting it.

'Are you looking forward to coming home?' I asked him, knowing that his week in the hospital was nearly up.

'I don't look forward anymore,' he said, with unexpected lucidity and I saw that he was watching me. 'Sometimes I hope,' he added.

He lay prone, his baleful eyes boring into mine. I sat and filled the time with memories of his long ago vigour and purpose. When it was time to go, I kissed him and said goodbye.

Outside, the patients still clogged the corridor. I passed on and rounded a corner, toying with metaphysical thoughts until the fearful eyes of a white-haired woman stopped me in my tracks.

'I'm lost,' she said, her voice half-strangled.

She was neatly dressed in dappled pink, an ironed, floral skirt flowed out from under a lilac cardigan, blue fur slippers cushioned her feet. But her frame trembled as I took her arm and led her on. I tried to channel my energy into our walk.

'I don't know what to do and I don't know where to go,' she whispered timidly, her face still pretty but riven with fear.

'You're not lost,' I told her but she remained unconvinced.

'My mother was lost. She was never found,' she continued, with great secrecy, and the echo of a truth seemed to hang like a cloud over the afternoon. As she stepped along nervously and we went towards the end of the corridor I feared the truth of what might have happened long ago.

'They couldn't find her,' she added, her voice nearly breaking. The white light of a sun-shower outside spilled across the ward and she grabbed hold of my hand.

'I'm eighty-five,' she confided. And in the flicker of her eyes I saw a mirror of my future life and glimpsed my own senility. As one, we walked in to an airy four-bedded ward.

'Here's your bed,' I told her. And ever so lightly she sat there, resting on its edge.

'I don't know where to go,' she pleaded, her face full of woe.

'Look at the lovely women here,' I told her, pointing at her fellow residents. 'They are all going to mind you.'

And in fairness, they smiled at us and waved and I left her and walked out into the evening, the damp air creeping up my arms as I left the warmth behind.

66

Dan, the Man

I'll never forget the morning the hurler Dan Shanahan came to our house in Ring to deliver the oil. It was in 2008, the year the Waterford hurlers made a bid to win the Liam MacCarthy Cup against Kilkenny in the All-Ireland final in Croke Park. Of course, RoseAnn had hinted to the receptionist in Comeragh Oil that we'd especially love if the hurling hero were the person to be despatched from the depot to make the delivery.

The day was still fine and the sun was making an early showing when he arrived. RoseAnn raced up the stairs in a flurry of excitement.

'Dan Shanahan is here with the oil,' she shouted incredulously. It was better than having a film star or a pop star come to call. We were out the door like greyhounds.

Dan Shanahan is revered in west Waterford. His prowess on the hurling field was undisputed. He was a gazelle on the pitch. He was grace and power, fire and skill, all rolled into one. He was a wizard with a hurl. He had always been the first player you would spot on the pitch. No one scored or ignited a crowd to the great levels of excitement like he could. In Dungarvan town, middle-aged women smiled with admiring nods when he passed. Men saluted him with a congratulatory shake of the head and a comradely 'Well, Dan the Man.' Young boys, and sometimes girls, nudged each other when he went by. Simply put, he was a celebrity in the Déise.

RoseAnn and I both ran to the back of the house like mad women, hyperventilating and foolish. I patted down my uncombed hair and, with my bed socks, corduroy skirt and torn jumper, hoped I didn't look like a character out of *Dancing at Lughnasa*. The giddy confusion I felt at the idea of meeting Dan Shanahan took me by surprise. Who knew I'd be so star-struck, or act so like a schoolgirl?

He was at our wall, standing tall by the lorry in all his handsome glory, the smile intact, the eyes full of vitality, the big hands hanging empty.

We were hardly able to talk such was our joy at meeting the man from Lismore. Over the years we'd seen him play in Semple Stadium against Limerick, against Cork, against Clare. We'd locked up and left parishes deserted to go and cheer for the men in blue and white. We'd travelled with neighbours, bedecked in the Waterford colours, to away matches when potential heartache battled it out with the sliver of a chance of victory. We'd seen the team defeated in Croke Park when we stood in the rain, soaked and disbelieving.

But whatever the match, when Dan raced up the field, it was time to jump to your feet. Pulses quickened when Dan moved. He was like lightning, swinging the hurley in a single flowing swirl of force. It was like watching a great ballet when his fellow team-mate, the great John Mullane – quick as a flash on thin white legs – got possession of the *sliotar* and passed it seamlessly to Shanahan. On those days of championship games, goals and points would rain thick and fast. The players would veer like greyhounds and they'd send the ball flying under or over the goalposts.

We always roared and cheered on Dan and the men. As he

stood there on the road that day beside the oil lorry, unassuming and soft-spoken, he chatted to us about Waterford's chances in that year's championship. At that stage, the team had yet to play Tipperary in the All-Ireland semi-final.

'Ye haven't peaked yet and that's good,' said I, like a seasoned commentator. He listened and nodded indulgently. Up close, he seemed so young and slight. Not the great beefy giant I had imagined. We swelled with pride as he chatted to us.

'Keep the prayers up,' he said.

'We will,' we assured him. And with a smile, he climbed into the cab of the lorry and he was gone.

On that morning at home, our hopes were high but caution and past defeats held our hearts in check. The heady excitement of possibly playing in an All-Ireland final – the first in forty-five years – had yet to lift us to new, dizzier heights.

A decade later, the idea of winning the All-Ireland is still only a dream. But my heart always rose up with pride when Dan lifted the ball onto his hurley. Time slowed down. All of us in the stands seemed to breathe as one – exhaling as the ball inevitably flew over the bar.

Even after the disappointment of the team's defeat in the All-Ireland final of 2008 – and again in 2017 with Dan on the sideline, as passionate as ever – I'm confident that with all the great Waterford men from around the county on our side, men who grew up admiring stars like Dan Shanahan, the Déise will surely be set to go all the way some day soon.

67

Nudes

Years ago, when I was teaching in Tipperary, I joined a painting class in nearby Limerick. On cold Tuesday nights we'd gather on the first floor of a cavernous room in a tall Georgian building somewhere along The Crescent. Our boots would make an awful racquet as we walked in across the bare wooden floorboards.

Then we'd take up our positions in front of the easels ranged around in a circle, brushes at the ready like guns in our hands, and a slim girl wrapped in a satin robe would walk in. She'd sit on a chair on a little plinth in our midst in front of a two-bar heater and wait for our instructor to give her the nod. After she'd composed herself, she'd untie the sash and allow her robe to fall open. There was an aura of mystery about the model's remote presence that left us amateur artists in a state of perpetual tension and incomprehension. We struggled with the form – the angle of her foot, the slope of her arm, the tilt of her head.

Ten years later I attended a different life-drawing class one summer when I was on holidays, this time in Cork. Each day I'd travel on a bus from Douglas, where I was staying with RoseAnn, and go into the city centre. I'd walk up along the River Lee to the Crawford College of Art, passing under the shadow of St Fin Barre's Cathedral and every morning I'd stand at an easel with a group of fellow painters learning how to paint. I remember that summer of charcoal smudges and greasy fingers, oil-smeared clothes and the reawakening of my vocational zeal to paint.

Again the model remained aloof and private, and her cool remoteness was like a challenge to me, seeing her there, a person who was unknowable, a being I was meant to paint or to sketch, to address only her outward form.

We did speed drawings with charcoal when we had to do a sketch in less than sixty seconds, and another rapid response in less than thirty seconds and finally we did quick-as-lightning ones in ten seconds or less. We were shocked by the accuracy of these attempts as we drew lines that flowed with grace and ease. It was an exercise that made our hands loose extensions of our emotional responses to the nude. Freeing our minds, which were trapped by logic and rational thought, we learned to let go of geometry and trust our instincts, trust the feeling of the line, of the curve. We had to make that visceral connection and draw a line by taking a leap of faith in our own instinctive response.

Those days have all but disappeared from my memory now. My drawings of nudes in charcoal, acrylics, oil and pencil are rolled up in a bundle on top of a wardrobe in the back room here in Ring. I opened them recently and saw their disproportionate limbs, their hips like Ben Bulben, their flesh that is sausage pink and garish, dipping wildly into recesses that are red and orange and brown. Why did I keep these misshapen representations of women who sat in remote stillness while I tried to draw what was in front of my eyes?

Soon my nudes will curl in a flame on a fire or perhaps some will stare out at me from an opaque recycling bag and I'll see their recriminatory hues of yellows and orange in shredded flashes. After they've evaporated into nothingness, all those hours from that summer in Cork will be gone. Layers of my life will peel away and the torn parts of paintings from that winter in Limerick will peep through a clear plastic bag.

I remain inert now, waiting, wondering why I stood at an easel to paint. My paints are shut away. I don't take them out. I am like the model in front of the two-bar heater, waiting for the time to pass, while others set out to draw, brushes at the ready.

68

The SS *Kincora*

Our painting of the SS *Kincora* remained unloved for years, hidden in the back room until RoseAnn and my mother took it to a restoration artist. When we saw the beautiful old oil painting come to life in all its glory, our curiosity was tweaked. What was the story behind this turn-of-the-century Steam Ship *Kincora*?

She was built in 1895 by Hawthorn, Leslie & Co, of Newcastle in England and owned by the Malcomsons of Waterford city. She plied her trade between Limerick and Liverpool, carrying general cargo, occasionally calling on the homeward or outward journey to Fenit or Galway. She was a fine 230-foot vessel, a steel screw steamer grossing nearly 1,000 tonnes. She had a 32-foot beam and a depth of 14.5 feet.

There is something tantalising about this modest painting. Perhaps it's the fact that the *Kincora* was just a working coastal steamship, with one funnel and back-up sails, fore and aft: she's not showy and her sturdy lines hint at the nature of the men who worked on board, ordinary decent men from Limerick, Waterford and Liverpool.

The artist, J. Bourne, who painted her was one of those painters who used to set up his easel at the end of the pier in Liverpool and paint the various ships that passed in or out in the hope of selling his work to captains who took pride in their vessels. Captain Edward Power, from Tramore in County Waterford, was captain of the *Kincora*. He must have liked the painting, purchased it from this pier-head painter and taken it home to hang on his wall. We don't know how it came to be in our possession, but we thought it was possible Captain Power may have known our grandfather, who was a river pilot on the River Suir, and had given it to him at some stage.

As we continued to uncover her history, we learned that the *Kincora* was lost after only six years in service. On her last morning, she was steaming along off the south coast of Ireland, away from the port of Limerick on her way to Liverpool, carrying a cargo of hay and one paying passenger. It was not long after midnight, in the early hours of Thursday 8 August 1901, when she was passing the Tuskar Rock just off the coast of County Wexford. There was dense fog when the giant-sized ocean liner, the *Oceanic*, as if out of the blue, came across her bows. The White Star Line ship was on her way to New York with 1,200 passengers on board. In spite of both ships using their foghorns, a collision occurred with fatal results for the *Kincora* and seven of the crew.

There was just enough time for ropes and ladders to be thrown down to the little steamship. Some of the survivors used these to come aboard. Two lifeboats were also put out by the *Oceanic*. Fourteen men, including Captain Power and ten of his crew, two stowaways and the ship's one paying passenger, a Mr J. Toppin from Limerick, were hauled aboard. Of the others, there was no trace.

One of those who perished was George Collins, a fire stoker, who went back down below in an act of heroism to turn off the boiler and prevent it from exploding. He left his wife and seven children destitute in Windmill Street in Limerick. But it's believed his bravery prevented the *Kincora* from blowing up under the port bow of the *Oceanic*. Had that happened, she would have caused much greater damage.

Within seven minutes, the ship was gone. The *Oceanic* waited and searched until dawn. As the day came up the great liner continued on to Queenstown. Once she'd berthed, the surviving men were left ashore.

Three months later the Admiralty Court ruled, finding that both ships had been proceeding at immoderate and excessive speeds. No real blame was ever apportioned.

But, at home, we wondered about the drowned sailors and the broken ship that was lying on the seabed. Eventually, we convinced TG4 to commission a documentary about the ship and so RoseAnn began digging further. During her research one day, out of the blue, she learned that a body had been washed up along the coast of Wexford, just beside Fethard-on-Sea, some three weeks after the ship went down. She uncovered the inquest report. The coroner's court had established that Charles Sacht, of Byron Street in Liverpool, was a member of the crew of the *Kincora*. We then learned that his family had never come over to claim his body. They never knew he was buried in Fethard-on-Sea until RoseAnn contacted them 100 years after the tragedy.

And so on a grey, overcast day we drove to the little village of Fethard-on-Sea and the picturesque church of St Mogue's to meet the descendants of Charles Sacht when they travelled over from Liverpool to pay their respects. The rooks were swooping down over the headstones when we walked down to his unmarked grave. That's where we stood, remembering the tragedy that took place on 8 August 1901 when the *Kincora* sank and seven men lost their lives.

69

Romance in the Air

It was dark and cold outside. Ice covered the roads and the sky was heavy with snow. Very few were out that night. There were just three men drinking at the counter in the Seanachie Bar, a place where I had worked when I was nineteen. The three bachelors were simply having a quiet drink in the dead of winter. RoseAnn and I sat at a table by the window. I ordered our drinks and we sat near the bar. Soon we were part of the company and they were talking to us.

One of them, a dark-eyed, thin man, sketched us a story of unrequited love. It was his own story but he brushed it off lightly, as if broken hearts were meant to be lived with and endured. He'd lost in love, he said. Thoughts of romance trembled on the air. I looked at this gaunt, lonely man and I recalled a couple I used to serve in the pub.

The two of them came in at 9 p.m. every week. Their whispered imprecations and concerned entreaties at the door always created a certain awed expectancy. Once they pushed through that heavy squeaking door heads began to turn to view their progress.

They were big people who moved slowly, cumbersomely even. Their bodies seemed to sway elegantly from side to side as they came down along the narrow bar, step by careful step. They seemed to mimic the great milking beasts of the farm where they spent their lives. Arriving at the counter, they would stand

and wait for me to serve them. There was a definite aura of glee about the pair of them. Although well into their middle years, they were newly wed.

Her face would light up at the sight of me and she'd bend her head slightly to one side and smile with pleasure when I went to take their order. He would stand slightly behind her in the bar's darkened passageway. He'd come close if she looked to him to furnish an answer. Even I, in my blinkered state of youthful indifference, could see he was a handsome man with a fine mouth, smiling eyes and a manly bearing. He always wore a suit and a dark trilby with a short trim. They looked well together.

Her voice, deep and velvet-like, would caress me. 'Hello, Catherine. How are you?' I remember her warmth and friendliness. And it was clear she had taken pains to dress up for the occasion – with a dab of rouge reddening her cheeks and a garish line of lipstick along her mouth. Usually, she sported a military-style suit and she sometimes wore a hat, its netting pulled forward jauntily over her forehead. A paste brooch often decorated her lapel.

With all the wisdom of my nineteen years, I used to view this woman and her soft-spoken husband in a slightly pitying way. I thought her innocent and simple. But I kept these preconceptions to myself. So when she put her handbag on the counter, her eyes twinkling at me full of the fun and excitement of being out together for a drink, I didn't fully appreciate how happy she was in her newly married bliss or how beautiful and lovely she was.

She'd give me the order then: 'A pint of Guinness and a vodka and slimline tonic.' And she'd chat to me while I got the drinks.

She leaned in close one night to tell me about their romance. I don't think I believed her. Secretly I dismissed her story, thinking she was away with the fairies. But she told me how they'd lived on neighbouring farms until she wrote him a letter one day suggesting he call up to the house so they could talk about getting married. She asked a mutual neighbour to deliver the letter. That's how she proposed to the shy farmer and he accepted.

'I asked him to marry me,' she said, watching my reaction. 'I did,' she said, seeing my disbelief, her great rheumy eyes reflecting the light that bounced off all the bottles ranged along the shelves. She wanted me to know how well it had all worked out.

I asked the men at the counter if they remembered this couple. They nodded. They are both gone now, they said. The dark-eyed, thin man remained still, saying nothing at all.

'Do you know that she proposed to him?' one of them asked me. 'O, she wrote to him,' the man continued. 'She gave the letter to a neighbour who lived between the two of them. She wrote, asking him to call down to her so that they could discuss marriage.'

We all savoured the wonder of it.

'And do you know,' said the man at the counter, 'the man who delivered the letter was a bachelor too and he couldn't understand why she hadn't asked him.'

There was a pause. The dark-eyed, thin man gave a cough before he spoke.

''Twas I brought it down to him,' he said, quiet and shy with the admission. 'That's right, 'twas me,' he said, nodding. 'And she had no eyes for me at all.'

Romance in the Air

After a moment of silence, he laughed quietly. It seemed the passage of time had dulled the embarrassment he'd felt and he was able to look back at himself to a time when he had been younger, foolish and full of hope.

The rest of us sipped our drinks quietly, sensing his regret. We savoured the disclosure, knowing that he'd shared a secret with us. Love was in the air that night, as I recalled the couple who used to put on their finery to come to the pub for a drink, where they would twinkle in the gloaming, exuding happiness.

70

Following the Wren

My return to living at home full-time did throw up a couple of memorable opportunities. With the dawn of St Stephen's Day one year, a mad impulse saw us dressing in a mish-mash of old clothes to 'Follow the Wren'.

Our plan was to revive this old tradition, where grown-ups (and children, on occasion) took to the roads, paraded and sang their hearts out, purportedly with the intention of hunting a wren. In reality, though, we'd simply go from place to place, belt out a few songs, create a racket and generally have fun.

About seven of us gathered together that morning, all suitably attired and ready to march through the streets of any village we came across. We smeared paint on our faces and donned capes and shawls. One of us wore an oversized Crombie; another sported a fur. Between us we had a selection of musical instruments – namely, a bodhrán, a tin whistle and two African drums.

We left Ring and motored along narrow boreens going through the western recesses of County Waterford in search of all its hidden villages. We descended on any pub we came across, stopping in Grange, Kiely's Cross, Tour, Aglish, Clashmore and Old Parish.

Weary drinkers in Clashmore were just recovering from the bedlam of their village's annual hunt, the sound of braying horns and barking beagles dying away in the distance, when they were awoken from the mid-afternoon lull by us crashing in upon them. We sang like a marauding horde, helped along by our bodhrán, drums and tin whistle. They cast bleary eyes in our direction, gazing on us with looks of bemused tolerance when we launched into a raucous rendition of 'Anois ar Theacht an tSamhraidh', roaring out the chorus: 'Oró, sé do bheatha abhaile, anois ar theacht an tsamhraidh'.

In Villierstown we put our instruments away to have a drink.

As darkness fell, we trekked over a track that skirted the Goish river and tried to find a fabled ancient stone that was said to be a relic with druidic powers. Did we hope to harness some of its pagan energy that Stephen's night in the dark?

A lunar light washed over us as we went in single file up the glen. When we found the slab of ogham stone, the inky light of another world, *na síoga agus teacht an fhir dhuibh* – the world of the fairies and of the devil – pulled us in.

One girl, who was the poet amongst us, with her red hair flowing down her back, stepped up onto a stone, raised her hands aloft to the heavens and addressed the goddess of the earth. The power of the ancient druids seemed to flow into us and we breathed in the misty night air until it felt like a benediction.

Perhaps it was the hot whiskies we'd imbibed along the way but the night seemed to slow down and the moonlight was suddenly full of portent and potential. A sense of resolution and expectancy took hold of us. It began to feel as if we'd broken the back of the old year and were coasting towards a countdown and the dawn of a new year. In spite of the icy cold and the lateness of the hour, we were slow to pull away from that place.

Fairies on Woodstown Strand

We walked along Woodstown Strand:
It was twilight
when fairies flit from briar to bud.

Even as the sun went down and the evening grew chill
We slipped through a veil
And remembered how we played as children.

We heard the tide coming in,
And our feet going over tiny crunching shells
Sounded like voices from forty years before
rolling in off the waves.

And we became light like crystal
And easy in the breeze
Amazed at all our eyes could see
in the gloaming.

Graveyard

The grave is a riot of blooms: swathes of salvia, lavender, geraniums, fuchsia, hollyhocks and campanula wave endearingly in the sun when I walk up to the headstone with Deirdre Morrissey, a cousin from Dublin. I have to keep myself in check from opening my mobile phone and taking a picture to tweet.

We stop to reminisce and admire the flowers that cover the plot. I take joy in the lovely shrubs that we have growing there, not to mention the little birdbath and the terracotta box of African daisies and Roses of Sharon. I could so easily send an image of this out into cyber space such is my ease and familiarity with the place where my mother and father are now buried. My heart fills with warmth at the sight but I stop even as the delphiniums and daisies wink at me.

Maybe I'm too free and comfortable with these graves. Maybe I shouldn't be feeling this cosiness in the cemetery, I think, as we walk on through the sunlit graveyard to visit another family plot. I point to the headstones of those neighbours that my cousin may remember and she is charmed by my intimate knowledge and lonely for her own family members who are buried in a sprawling cemetery in the city.

She finds it all a far cry from her own urban existence where, she says, tragedy is usually borne anonymously and there is no comparable outpouring of communal grief after death strikes. At the removal of a soul from a country parish it seems everyone is pained and moved to sympathise, each person lining up to shake the hands of grieving family members.

As the sun throws dappled light across the grass, I lead my cousin along the path up through the graves and I wonder if I am seeing this place through rose-tinted glasses. And yet, our lives revolve to a greater or lesser extent around this place of tranquillity and we are drawn back here again and again, reminded of how life ends and how we are left with an existential silence.

Here lie individuals who leave loneliness and a lifetime of memories in their wake. Here lies a neighbour who came home from Hollywood with his family every summer to while away his time down on the pier fishing and boating. Here lies a devoted family man, who was passionate about his greyhounds and the Friday night race meets in Youghal. The graveyard is rich with the detail and intricacies of stories that have woven their way into my life. I remember them all as we walk along the path, an old tree casting welcome shade over us.

We turn a corner and walk up towards the leafy resting place of the skipper who went down with his crew in a tragic maritime accident not so long ago. Here is the elegantly maintained grave of the beautiful young girl who died in a freak accident on her way home in her car one night.

The place is quiet. It feels peaceful and comforting to walk among the stones, even as the men dig a grave for the young man who has just been killed, cut down in a road accident in the prime of his life. On the morning of his funeral, cars will stretch along both sides of the road for half a mile and more.

Was it mad to lie on my mother's grave when she was interred here first – three years before my father died – to see what she could see? Is it morbid or strange to feel such a connection with this place, where pain is public, where sorrow is a low *caoineadh*, where there are no answers? Yet sculpted stones record the dates and details of lives once lived. And as we walk I read the names and I remember who they were and where they lived and the knowledge of their lives buoys me up.

My cousin and I walk down to the gate. We sit in my car and drive home. I salute a neighbour who passes in his jeep. I watch a lorry ahead slow down to make the turn at the corner of Bóthar na Sop and Cnocán an Phaoraigh. I brake too to make the hill as we carry on home.

73

A Kaleidoscope of Days

On the pier
Looking back,
Through a kaleidoscope of days
And a swirl of high skies,
Time sweeps along
Over a tide of blue and grey
To a day when I was younger,
Braver and unsure.
I was a toddler first,
In toeless shoes,
And a morning-clean sundress with bloomers,
Standing in a garden of lobelia,
alongside the paddy-go-sleep.
Then I was an angel
in white gloves,
my First Holy Communion dress,
with rosary beads
rattling in my handbag.
They must have watched with baited breath
when I stepped forth to dazzle
and I sang a song
that curled around my listeners.
Then I was a grown-up in my first car.
When they waved me off

A Kaleidoscope of Days

I accelerated like a maniac.
In the doorway, picture perfect,
I see them still,
Not moving but standing
As if holding onto some pain
Until the moment of my arrival,
When I'd waltz in like a princess
To their welcome home.

74

When Walls Grow Cold

Attached to a wall in our sitting room is a storm lantern, secured in a brass bracket. The oil-fuelled lamp, which once stood in a lighthouse window, always reflects the firelight. It casts a warm glow around the room and sometimes, if you look into the reflection, the telescoped room seems to be humming or spinning as if in a zoetrope.

A good number of my mother's paintings hang on the walls of our sitting room. They feature ships and quays, shorelines, stormy seas and moonlit cliffs, dreamy scenes in rich tones of purples and orange, violet and greens.

There's a special painting of my father when he was a young man, sitting as the stroke of the maiden eight-man crew when they won the Gough Shield, rowing to victory along the River Suir in the 1940s. My mother did this painting for his eightieth birthday, her fingers barely able to hold the brush at the time. It still shimmers with light and life.

On another wall, there are family photographs of holy communions and weddings, of children and cousins, neighbours and friends all ranged in a patchwork of lines. Against the opposite wall is an old walnut sideboard that came with us from Lower Newtown. Inside this we keep bottles of port and sherry, sewing baskets, an old pair of binoculars, the willow pattern set of dinner plates and platters that only come out on special occasions and a range of old glass siphons and decanters that never see the light of day. Hanging overhead is the gorgeous red and turquoise painting by the artist Mick O'Dea that I have of myself staring into the future. This is the second portrait I have of myself that Mick O'Dea painted.

The fire always has to be lit in this room, especially on cold days, because the house in Ring is old and the place is freezing unless we have flames leaping up the chimney. We huddle round the fire at the centre of the house. Even in the summer, the fire is rarely let go out. The people who owned this house in the 1800s, long before my family came here, probably also had roaring fires.

After a few days away, the bleak coldness of the rooms always strikes me on our return, especially in the sitting room. Like the cold hand of death, there is a chill in the room after our absence and it can feel like a cave. This is mainly because the walls of our house are so wide, and these three-foot deep walls will hold the cold for days, or years if we leave them. The doorways are all set in deep recesses. They go as deep as the length of a man's arm, a recess that's as engulfing and unfathomable as the memory of an embrace.

In the hall, a staircase leads up to the bedrooms upstairs. It is an unusually steep and narrow stairs. Often, as I take the stairs two at a time, I fancy I could be living in the Himalayas where the traditional mountain homes of Nepal and Tibet have stairs like ladders built on the outside of their walls.

RoseAnn and I, who live here now, are used to the odd eccentricities of this old, two-storey house. Miriam, who lives nearby, is often here too. Each of us knows its creaks and cracks, its flaws and foibles, its wainscoted walls and rattling windows. We know its skylight views and its creaking ceilings, which draw the eye upwards in wonderment when a tiny movement overhead might be a mouse or some other little creature running over the rafters.

We've lived our lives in and around these rooms but when we are gone, the stone walls will still be here. The walls stand quietly, asleep, while the fire is lighting. And they will stand silently there, solid, like sleeping sentries when the fire goes out.

Today our walls are decked out with our photos and paintings, but once our stories have dried up, once the grate is empty and the teapot has gone stony cold on the hearth, they will slowly take on the touch of damp and the cold clamminess of a corpse. Then mould and flaking paint will appear and rotten wood and mushroom smells will take hold. When the fire goes out, a creeping chill will begin and all you'll hear will be the lonely echo of our forgotten voices.

The walls – stoic, stolid, suspicious and stark – will stay shtum. There will be no sounds. There will be no fire, no talk, only the silent freeze of emptiness. When there is no one here to light the fire, the damp will start to seep in and decay will come creeping.

75

Midnight Mass

Attending the Midnight Mass on Christmas Eve has been a tradition in our family since my childhood in Ring, a tradition we uphold to this day. Every year follows a similar pattern.

We sprinkle our whispers like sugar on a cake as we crunch over the frosty stones on our way in through the gates to the chapel: 'Nollaig Shona dhaoibh' – *Happy Christmas* – and 'Conas a thá sibh?' – *How are ye?*

The church is on a hill overlooking the sea, which is inky black and mysterious at night-time, its waters slipping over rocks that are way down, hidden out of earshot but a presence still in all our minds.

'Tá sé fuar,' we add – *it's cold.*

'Ó, tá sé an-fhuar,' we hear in response. *Oh, it's very cold.*

Then we are likely to hear a question to a young person from Mona Breathnach, who was a primary school teacher in Ring and knows all about children and their main focus of attention around Christmas time: 'An bhfuil Daidí na Nollag ag teacht?' *Is Santa coming?*

As we reach the porch, we bless ourselves at the holy water font, nod to each other and go inside. The darkened lights of midnight always give the vaulted church a ghostly feel, as if all in heaven are present, watching us with baited breath. With night-lights on the altar and in the crib, as well as flickering candles around the chapel, the interior seems to heave like the sea and we become aware of the heavens beyond the stained-glass windows rearing high into space. Everything feels medieval and mysterious.

Huddles of families, returned relatives, rarely seen neighbours and maybe a once-upon-a-time heart-throb, file into the pews in the chapel at midnight. The hush is deafening while we wait, clearing our throats, un-belting our new coats, knocking against kneelers, fumbling with our car keys.

Us girls have always tripped across to join the choir, squeezing into the pew beside our neighbours and fellow choristers, Saidí Breathnach and Alice Ciuliú, for our annual get-together. There are twinkling eyes and knowing smiles all around as we study the hymn books and try to remember what we'd sung the year before.

'Cad é an chéad cheann?' I ask – *What's the first one?* – and word comes back along the seat, directing me to 'uimhir a fiche trí, "Don Oíche úd i mBeithil"' – *number 23, 'For That Night in Bethlehem'.*

Before the priest comes out to the altar, there might be just enough time to scan the faces in the congregation and remember those who were no longer there – my own mother and father, Joe, Sheila, Gile, Breandán, Hannie, Bean Breathnach.

When the priest emerges he begins with the blessing: 'In ainm an Athair, 's an Mhic, 's an Spioraid Naoimh, Amen.' *In the name of the Father, the Son and the Holy Spirit.* When he gives us the look, we straighten up, clear our throats and wait for the signal from Moya Bean Uí Dhomhnaill, who sits at the organ. Then, unevenly at first, with pages rustling, we put our giddiness aside and sing.

Being in the choir at Midnight Mass was better than Broadway. I had always been a member until I went away to study and work. Still, when I was home on holidays, I was able to join in for special festive occasions such as Easter and Christmas. In readiness for those special Masses, we'd be corralled into order and I'd attend a flurry of last-minute rehearsals. On my full-time return to Ring I'd once again joined the choir.

On the night of Christmas, we always steal the show. Our hearts swell when our voices rise up to fill the old church with the sound.

> Don oíche úd i mBeithil,
> beidh tagairt ar ghrian go brách,
> don oíche úd i mBeithil
> go dtáinig an Bréithear slán …
>
> *For that night in Bethlehem,*
> *A night as bright as dawn,*
> *For that night in Bethlehem,*
> *When the word was born.*

Afterwards, we sit back, satisfied, our breaths slow, thoughts swirling around in our heads, conjuring up images of angels and stars, shepherds and donkeys, and all the souls who floated above our heads. And I'd begin, as always, to submit to the chanting and soothing pattern of the Mass.

The ceremony seems to calm the chaos. Time stands still as we listen to the tinkling of the wine being poured into the chalice, our minds so heightened that we can almost swear to hearing the frost settling on the headstones outside.

It was usually about midway through the celebrations that the much-loved voice of Nioclás Tóibín used to break like a trumpet through the church. Like a mighty zephyr, he filled the vaulted chapel with lovely, clear notes. He usually stood in one of the pews near the back of the church with all the other parishioners. The sound was enough to make the hair stand on the back of your neck. He rang like a bell, tolling the ages, without any accompaniment. You'd see him if you looked back, his chest out, his head back and his eyes looking up, like a boy still, proud that he was singing 'Ár nAthair atá sna flaithis go hard' – *Our Father who is in Heaven.*

His notes seemed to gather momentum, like a rising wave, holding on for the thrilling finish to come. It was as if a general absolution washed over all of us when Nioclás carried us in that cradle of sound. It drew us down a tunnel of memory to long ago when ancestors worshipped the dawn or *bandia na gréine* – the sun goddess. We seemed to sway like reeds in a breeze, spellbound. Then his voice took us down the slow lyrical descent in a plea for freedom from death, for salvation, 'ach saor sinn ó bhás, anam Chríost' – *but save us from death, soul of Christ* – as we rose and fell like the tide on the power of his resonating notes.

There was nowhere to look after he finished singing. Some of us seemed almost afraid to share the moment, to acknowledge shyly the mystical quality of the Mass and so look inwards. There can be no doubt that every Christmas the singing of Nioclás Tóibín calmed our hearts.

These days, after the ceremony, we drive home, passing the grotto, flying up Bothar na Sop, past the *meánscoil*, and down the old road to Baile na nGall.

As we near home, I think of my mother and father and how they loved Christmas, and how my father always sang the 'Adeste' with such exuberance and joy.

Midnight Mass

When I stand on the headland at Ceann a Bhathla, I'll remember all those who have gone. I'll see them sparkling on the waves in the moonlight off Mine Head, floating towards heaven, drifting towards dawn. All night I'll dream I am travelling towards them, until morning when I wake and it's Christmas and they have gone. But Nioclás will be singing and the souls will be twinkling, like stars in the firmament, watching over me while the sun rises.

Acknowledgements

My family has always been at the heart of what and when, where and how I write. An abiding memory I have is of my father dashing around upstairs before any of us were up, looking for a tape recorder so that he could record one of my pre-recorded stories that was about to be broadcast on the radio. (This was long before podcasts!) He and my mother always encouraged me to write and they loved hearing me on the radio. There was great jubilation in our house if I was in the line-up any Sunday morning just after 9 a.m. when the long-running RTÉ Radio 1 series *Sunday Miscellany* aired.

Over the years, going out to the RTÉ studios to record my stories under the guidance and gentle direction of Clíodhna Ní Anluain, when she was producer of *Sunday Miscellany*, was always a thrilling and a nurturing experience. Clíodhna played a key role in helping me understand how I could become a better storyteller. I am thrilled that subsequent producers, namely Aoife Nic Cormaic and Sarah Binchy, continue to broadcast my stories, while Eileen Heron and Aonghus McAnally also showcased my stories during their time at the helm. I also worked with Fionnuala Hayes and Geralyn Aspill, the programme's broadcasting co-ordinators. What writer could ask for more than to be able to read their own work to the programme's devoted listeners?

Down the years there have been so many good people who have helped me develop as a writer. I'm indebted in particular to Marie Murray, Monica McInerney, Máire Seó Breathnach,

Acknowledgements

Christine Monk, Marie O'Halloran, Jack Harte, Jack Gilligan, Eibhlín de Paor, Margaret Organ, Grace Wells and in particular the late great Ella Shanahan, who was a fellow Waterford woman and my unofficial mentor in *The Irish Times*. I've learned a lot from many former colleagues, contemporaries and friends in journalism, but it is Ella who came back from her posting as the paper's London editor and took me under her wing.

Those who have read my work and encouraged me along the way are Michael Coady, Micheal O'Siadhail, Anthony Glavin, Liam Carson and Maura O'Kiely, who published my first story, 'The Helvick Summer', in *U Magazine* back in 1992. I'm also grateful to the late Mairéad Ní Chinnéide, who was editor of my two first Irish language books.

Others who have encouraged me include Colette Sheridan, my cousins Deirdre Morrissey and Donal Musgrave, as well as Donal's wife Shirley and my nephew Joseph Foley, who is my technical consultant and has always been on hand to sort out any laptop or Internet issues I might have. I'd also like to thank him – along with my sisters Miriam and RoseAnn, and my brother-in-law, George Macleod – for their support and love.

ALSO AVAILABLE FROM MERCIER PRESS

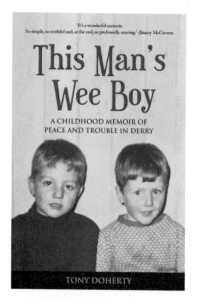

ISBN: 978 1 78117 458 6

Set against the background of the growing tensions between residents, the dreaded 'B-men' and the British Army, Tony Doherty skilfully paints a picture of life in a working-class family, the local characters on his street and the joys and tribulations of a child growing up in a city on the verge of civil war.

Tony's father, Patsy, is central to the story – a legend in his son's eyes and a man who struggles to raise a family through bitter years of economic inactivity. This is an emotive, laugh-out-loud funny and, at times, heartbreakingly sad portrayal of Tony's relationship with the father he adores, yet slightly fears, right up to a bitterly cold January afternoon when the conflict changes Tony and his family's life forever.

www.mercierpress.ie

ALSO AVAILABLE FROM MERCIER PRESS

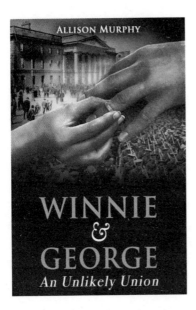

ISBN: 978 1 78117 470 8

Maria Winifred 'Winnie' Carney and George McBride came from different backgrounds and lived opposing lives. She was a Roman Catholic. He belonged to the Church of Ireland. She was a republican. He was a unionist. She was a member of Cumann na mBan. He had been in the loyalist Young Citizen Volunteers group. She became James Connolly's secretary and carried a Webley gun in the GPO during the Easter Rising. He fought for the British Army at the Somme during the Great War. *Winnie & George* tells the true and previously untold story of two individuals who lived remarkable lives and formed a very unlikely union. It is a powerful lesson in how love, once discovered, can be greater than the sum of all our divisions.

www.mercierpress.ie

MERCIER PRESS

IRISH PUBLISHER - IRISH STORY

We hope you enjoyed this book.

Since 1944, Mercier Press has published books that have been critically important to Irish life and culture. Books that dealt with subjects that informed readers about Irish scholars, Irish writers, Irish history and Ireland's rich heritage.

We believe in the importance of providing accessible histories and cultural books for all readers and all who are interested in Irish cultural life.

Our website is the best place to find out more information about Mercier, our books, authors, news and the best deals on a wide variety of books. Mercier tracks the best prices for our books online and we seek to offer the best value to our customers.

Sign up on our website to receive updates and special offers.

www.mercierpress.ie
www.facebook.com/mercier.press
www.twitter.com/irishpublisher

Mercier Press, Unit 3b, Oak House, Bessboro Rd, Blackrock, Cork, Ireland